MW00776322

MIDDLE EAST

DR. ANDY WOODS

DISPENSATIONAL
PUBLISHING HOUSE, INC.

Printed in the United States of America

First Edition, First Printing, 2016

ISBN: 978-1-945774-00-3

Dispensational Publishing House, Inc.
220 Paseo del Pueblo Norte
Taos, NM 87571

www.dispensationalpublishing.com

Ordering Information:
Quantity sales. Special discounts are available on quantity purchases by churches, associations, and others. For details, contact the publisher at the address above.

Orders by U.S. trade bookstores and wholesalers. Please contact the publisher:
Tel: (855) 437-9448

1 2 3 4 5 6 7 8 9 10

This book is dedicated to Ursula Kemp, who has both a remarkable testimony and also ministry. Because of her faithfulness in teaching both women and children in home and church Bible studies, she has had a transgenerational influence upon the city of Houston.

I remain in deep appreciation for not only her personal encouragement to me in ministry but also for her many hours of Biblically astute proofreading to my writings. I am honored to call her a Sugar Land Bible Church member. More importantly, I am honored to call her my personal friend.

Table of Contents

Introduction

In this book entitled *The Middle East Meltdown* we are going to focus our attention on the famous prophecy found in Ezekiel 38 and 39. However, it's a meltdown only from the human point of view, not the Divine perspective. A subtitle for this material is *The Coming Islamic Invasion of Israel*. There is a very fascinating Chinese saying that states, "May You Live in Interesting Times." I think the time period that we are living in now would qualify as interesting. Given the choice, there is not a time period in history that I would rather be living in than now. Why? The Lord seems to be setting the stage for His return as never before. One of these major stage-setting trends that we are currently seeing is the rise of a coalition of nations that harbors a hostile intent toward Israel. No matter which presidential administration comes into office in this nation and no matter how the calendar turns, this is an issue that does not seem to go away.

The prophet Ezekiel foresaw these things 2,600 years ago in a vision along the Chebar River (Ezek. 1:3) in Babylon. Ezekiel is one of two exilic prophets.

As a contemporary of Daniel, he prophesied during the days of the Babylonian Captivity, when the nation of Israel was in exile 350 miles removed from its land in a place called Babylon. Galatians 4:4, records, "When the fullness of time came, God sent forth His Son." As regards to the first coming of Jesus Christ, Jesus could not have entered history at any time. He had to come on God's timetable, at a specific instant called the "fullness of time," which was an era marked by the following characteristics:

- The Greek language was the dominant language of that time. This language is one of the richest and fullest dialects known to man. Thus, by the time that Jesus was born into the world, the Greek language was already in place for the proper recording of the revelation of God's Son.

- It was a period called *Pax Romana,* which refers to universal peace under Roman rule.

- A safe network of Roman roads was in place as well.

- Thus, circumstances were perfect for the recording of the revelation of Jesus Christ and the rapid transmission of the gospel. Besides, Christ entered human history during a time of heightened Messianic expectation (cf. Luke 3:15). Therefore, Jesus was placed into the world at the exact and right time.

Now, if that is all true for the first coming of Christ, it stands to reason that God is currently setting the world stage for the second coming of Christ. When you go and watch a basketball game and the teams come out and do layup drills, when they start selling popcorn, and the bleachers fill up with fans, you know that something is about ready to start—a basketball game. In the same way, God is orchestrating things in our world for the end-time drama. Ezekiel 38 and 39 represent key chapters that help us comprehend the direction in which our world is currently moving. We will deal with these prophetically significant chapters from two angles.

First, we will ask *five* standard journalistic questions about these chapters. *Second,* we will examine *seven* points of application.

CHAPTER

I

Who?

L et us begin with the journalistic questions. Typical journalistic
questions are: "Who?", "When?", "Why?", "What?" and "How?"[1]
First, *who* is involved in this end-time drama? Second, *when*
will these events happen? Third, *why* is it happening? In other words,
what is the overarching motive of these nations attacking Israel in the
last days? Fourth, *what* are the aftereffects or the outcome of these
things? Fifth, *how* is the world stage currently being set up for the
fulfillment of these events?

Following this analysis, we will then conclude with *seven* points
of application.

Let us begin with the *who* question.

---

1 I am indebted to Mark Hitchcock for this structure. See Mark Hitchcock, "The
Battle of Gog and Magog," <http://www.pre-trib.org/data/pdf/Hitchcock-TheBat-
tleofGogandMag.pdf>; Internet; accessed 20 May 2015.

Ezekiel 38:1–7 states:

> And the word of the LORD came to me saying, "Son of man, set your face toward Gog of the land of Magog, the prince of Rosh, Meshech and Tubal, and prophesy against him and say, 'Thus says the Lord GOD, "Behold, I am against you, O Gog, prince of Rosh, Meshech and Tubal. I will turn you about and put hooks into your jaws, and I will bring you out, and all your army, horses and horsemen, all of them splendidly attired, a great company *with* buckler and shield, all of them wielding swords; Persia, Ethiopia and Put with them, all of them *with* shield and helmet; Gomer with all its troops; Beth-togarmah *from* the remote parts of the north with all its troops—many peoples with you. Be prepared, and prepare yourself, you and all your companies that are assembled about you, and be a guard for them.""'

We find nine names mentioned here. They are *Magog, Rosh, Meshech, Tubal, Persia, Put, Cush, Gomer* and *Togarmah*. Now, none of these names can be found in a contemporary newspaper. Our knowledge of these names goes back to Genesis 10, which is a record of the Table of Nations. This chapter records where Noah's descendants settled following the flood and national dispersion at the Tower of Babel. Most of these names (*Magog, Rosh, Meshech, Tubal, Gomer* and *Togarmah*) come from the lineage of Noah's son Japheth (Gen. 10:2–3). Two of them, *Cush* and *Put*, are descendants of another of Noah's sons whose name was Ham (Gen. 10:6). Ezekiel is obviously not using names from the 21st century. Rather, he is using names from his own day back in the sixth century B.C. If we simply track where these people groups had settled in the general time of Ezekiel (593–573 B.C.) and then locate the corresponding modern nations and geographical areas, we can identify the nations that will invade Israel in the last days according to Ezekiel's prophecy.

We can do this analysis by consulting scholarly sources. One such source that is helpful in this regard is a first-century Jewish-Roman

NINE NATIONS OF EZEKIEL 38:1-7

1. *Magog*
2. *Rosh*
3. *Meshech*
4. *Tubal*
5. *Persia*
6. *Put*
7. *Cush*
8. *Gomer*
9. *Togarmah*

historian by the name of Josephus, who wrote a book called *Antiquities*. In 1.6.1 and 1.6.2 of *Antiquities*, Josephus provides a tremendous description of where these people groups and descendants of Noah eventually settled. Another resource that is equally helpful is the standard Hebrew lexicon by *Brown, Driver and Briggs (BDB)*. Herodotus, who authored *Histories* near the general time of Ezekiel in 450 B.C., is also helpful. Such material may seem a bit academic at first. However, this background is necessary because the opponents of the interpretation that I am going to provide typically seek to discredit this interpretation by arguing that it is the product of "newspaper exegesis." In other words, we are accused of just looking at present world events and then reading them back into the Bible. However, my goal is to demonstrate that this interpretation is not the product of "newspaper exegesis." Rather, the location of all of these names and nations that Ezekiel recorded can be documented from scholarly sources.

Magog

The first name mentioned by Ezekiel is *Magog*. Josephus identifies *Magog* as the Scythians, saying "Magog founded those that from him were named Magogites, but who are by the Greeks called Scythians."[2] Any encyclopedia will tell you that the Scythians migrated from central Asia to southern Russia around the eighth to the seventh century B.C. So I believe that the Scythians represent the nations of central Asia. These nations would represent the various "stans," such as Kazakhstan and Afghanistan, as well as the Ukraine.

Rosh

We come to a second nation mentioned, named *Rosh*. Let's consider the words of Gesenius. Who is Gesenius? Gesenius is the father of modern-day lexicography, which is the science and art of compiling Hebrew dictionaries. Consequently, Gesenius obviously carries credibility

---

2 Josephus, *Antiquities*, 1.6.1.

as a first-rate Hebrew scholar. He did a study of 10th-century Byzantine writers. Consequently, he believed that *Rosh* settled in what we call modern-day Russia. Gesenius observed, "pr. n. of a northern nation, mentioned with *Tubal* and *Meshech*; undoubtedly the *Russians*, who are mentioned by the Byzantine writers of the tenth century, under the name the *Ros*, dwelling to the north of Taurus . . . as dwelling on the river Rha (*Wolga*)."[3] Gesenius obviously cannot be accused of newspaper exegesis since he reached this conclusion prior to his death in 1842. This early date was long before the communist revolution in Russia and long before the rise (and subsequent collapse) of the modern Soviet Union as a nuclear superpower. Thus, in Ezekiel's prophecy, *Rosh* is Russia.

Meshech and Tubal

Next, we run into two other names: *Meshech* and *Tubal*. The *New Scofield Reference Bible* locates these two nations in Moscow (or Russia) and Tobolsk (or Siberia). Scofield explained, "That the primary reference is to the northern (European) powers, headed up by Russia, all agree. . . .The reference to Meshech and Tubal (Moscow and Tobolsk) is a clear mark of identification."[4] The difficulty with this interpretation is that in Ezekiel 27:13 these two nations or people groups are mentioned. Ezekiel 27:13 states, "Javan, Tubal and Meshech, they were your traders; with the lives of men and vessels of bronze they paid for your merchandise." Thus, these two groups are in a trading relationship with Tyre in Ezekiel 27. Tyre is modern-day Lebanon. It's hard to believe that groups that far removed geographically from Lebanon and all the way North in Russia and Siberia, back in Ezekiel's time, could be in a trading relationship with Tyre. A better interpretation comes from Edwin Yamauchi, who identifies *Meshech* and *Tubal* as *Moschoi* and *Tibarenoi* (Greek writings) or *Musku*

---

3 Wilhelm Gesenius, *Gesenius' Hebrew and Chaldee Lexicon* (Samuel Bagster and Sons, 1847; reprint, Grand Rapids: Baker, 1987), p. 752.

4 C. I. Scofield, ed. *The New Scofield Reference Bible* (New York: Oxford University, 1909; reprint, 1996), p. 883.

and *Tabal* (Assyrian inscriptions) in modern-day Turkey.[5] Herodotus, who wrote about 450 B.C., corroborates Yamauchi's interpretation. In his work called *Histories*, in 3.93 and 3.94, and 7.78, Herodotus identifies *Meshech* and *Tubal* as a group of people living in the mountains southeast of the Black Sea, which would be modern-day Turkey.

BDB also identifies *Meshech's* location in Persian times. Keep in mind that the Persian times began just a few decades after the time of Ezekiel (593–573 B.C.) in 539 B.C. *BDB* identifies *Meshech* in Persian times living southeast of the Black Sea,[6] which also would be modern-day Turkey. Josephus identifies *Meshech* as Cappadocia, explaining, ". . . and the Mosocheni were founded by Mosoch; now they are Cappadocians."[7] Cappadocia is mentioned in 1 Peter 1:1 as one of the locations to which Peter wrote—a place where scattered believers resided in north-central Turkey. *BDB* also equates *Tubal* with Cappadocia.[8] Thus, *Meshech* and *Tubal* are most likely modern-day Turkey.

Persia

The fifth name mentioned here is *Persia*. *Persia* is probably the easiest nation to identify because *Persia* has a paper trail. We know about the Medo-Persian Empire through Daniel's prophecies (cf. Dan. 2:39a; 5:28; 8:20; 10:13, 20). The Persians are a group of people that were predicted to become the second nation to trample down Israel during the Times of the Gentiles (Dan. 2; 7). In Daniel's sixth-century predictions, Medo-Persia was represented by the chest and arms of silver of the statue in Daniel 2, the bear of Daniel 7, and the ram of

---

5 Edwin Yamauchi, *Foes from the Northern Frontier* (Grand Rapids: Baker, 1982), pp. 24–27.
6 Francis Brown, S. R. Driver and Charles A. Briggs, eds., *A Hebrew and English Lexicon of the Old Testament: With an Appendix Containing the Biblical Aramaic* (Oxford: Clarendon Press, 1907), p. 604.
7 Josephus, *Antiquities*, 1.6.1.
8 Brown, Driver, and Briggs, eds., p. 1063.

Daniel 8. Medo-Persia overthrew the Babylonians in 539 B.C. as per Daniel 5, which is the chapter that details the account of the handwriting on the wall.

Interestingly, the Persians were the "good guys" around the time of Ezekiel. Just a few decades after this it was under the decree of the Persian ruler Cyrus that Judah was allowed to return to its homeland after the 70 years of captivity (2 Chron. 36:22–23; Ezra 1:1–4). What is striking to note is that about 150 to 200 years in advance of this, Isaiah the prophet called out Cyrus by name as Israel's future deliverer (Isa. 44:28–45:1). This is a staggering prediction. This would be like someone calling out the name of President Ronald Reagan 200 years ago, and predicting that he was going to be the future president of the United States, with that prophecy coming to pass. That is the precise equivalent of what we see in Isaiah's prophecy about Cyrus. Of course, miracle-rejecting liberals are so bothered by this that they have to take the book of Isaiah and chop it up in order to argue that Isaiah did not write that section involving the Cyrus prediction. Instead, according to these critical scholars, someone other than Isaiah, such as Deutero-Isaiah or Trito-Isaiah, allegedly wrote it long after the fact as a history lesson rather than a prediction. Liberals come to this conclusion only because they read the Bible with naturalistic presuppositions. As evangelicals, we have no problem accepting Isaiah's prophecy concerning Cyrus as predictive since we believe that there is a God who reveals "the end from the beginning" (Isa. 46:10).

In Ezekiel's time, the Persians were indeed the "good guys." In fact, all three Jewish returns from the Babylonian Captivity (as recorded in the books of Ezra and Nehemiah) took place under Persian kings. *Persia* continued on as a modern-day nation until *Persia's* name was changed to Iran in 1935. In 1979, during the presidency of Jimmy Carter, the nation was Islamicized and consequently renamed from Iran to the Islamic Republic of Iran. This occurred while America was suffering from long gas lines, when the Shah in Iran was deposed and replaced by the Ayatollah. Consequently, the climate of Iran began to change dramatically in 1979. In Ezekiel's prophecy *Persia* represents this modern state of Iran.

Cush

The next nation named by Ezekiel is *Cush*. In *The Antiquities of the Jews*, Josephus defines *Cush* as Ethiopia, explaining, "For of the four sons of Ham, time has not at all hurt the name of Cush; for the Ethiopians, over whom he reigned, are even at this day, both by themselves and by all men in Asia, called Cushites."[9] In fact, in Ezekiel 38:5, the New American Standard Bible uses the word "Ethiopia" as a translation of the Hebrew word "*Cush*." The *Ryrie Study Bible* indicates that the ancient country of Ethiopia encompassed far more territory than the modern country of Ethiopia, since the ancient country of Ethiopia included the northern Sudan.[10] The *Wycliffe Bible Encyclopedia* states under the entry "*Cush*": "The designation, Ethiopia, is misleading for it did not refer to the modern state of Ethiopia . . . Cush . . . bordered Egypt on the S[outh], . . . or modern Sudan."[11] Thus, *Cush* is most likely modern-day Sudan.

Put

Then we come to *Put*. In *BDB*, when you look up the Hebrew word *Put* it defines *Put* as Libya.[12] Josephus also defines *Put* as Libya.

> Phut also was the founder of Libya, and called the inhabitants Phutites, from himself: there is also a river in the country of Moors which bears that name; whence it is that we may see the greatest part of the Grecian historiographers mention that river and the adjoining country by the apellation of Phut: but the name it has now has been by change given it from one of the sons of Mesraim, who was called Lybyos.[13]

Thus, in Ezekiel 38:5, *Put* represents the modem country of Libya.

---

9   Josephus, *Antiquities*, 1.6.2.
10 Charles C. Ryrie, *Ryrie Study Bible: New American Standard Bible* (Chicago: Moody, 1995), p. 1,021.
11 Philip C. Johnson, "Cush," in *Wycliffe Bible Encyclopedia,* ed. Howard F. Vos, Charles F. Pfeiffer, John Rea (Chicago: Moody, 1975), p. 1.411.
12 Brown, Driver, and Briggs, eds., p. 806.
13 Josephus, *Antiquities*, 1.6.2.

Gomer

Now we come to the name *Gomer*. Josephus identifies *Gomer* as Galatia. He clarifies, "For Gomer founded those whom the Greeks now call Galatians, [Galls,] but were then called Gomerites."[14] Those familiar with the New Testament will immediately recognize the name Galatia since this was a people group that was the recipient of Paul's very first epistle. Galatia is also the area that Paul traveled through on his missionary journeys. Paul spent at least a year there on his first missionary journey. He then retraced his steps through Galatia on his second and third missionary journeys. Galatia is modern-day Turkey. Thus, *Gomer* is Galatia.

Togarmah

The last name mentioned on Ezekiel's list is *Togarmah*. Josephus equates *Togarmah* with Phrygia. He notes, ". . . Thrugramma the Thrugrammeans, who, as the Greeks resolved, were named Phrygians."[15] Acts 16:6 indicates that Paul traveled in Phrygia on his second missionary journey. This verse records, "They passed through the Phrygian and Galatian region, having been forbidden by the Holy Spirit to speak the word in Asia." Thus, Phrygia is the area between Galatia and Asia, which would also be modern-day Turkey. Therefore, *Togarmah* also should be equated with modern-day Turkey.

Summary

Now we can go through an academic process in order to specifically identify who the nations are as mentioned by Ezekiel even before we start examining present world events. Although it is acceptable to look at the headlines and see where we are in terms of the progress and development of the prophetic scenario, a problem materializes when we do not examine

---

14   Ibid., 1.6.1.
15   Ibid.

the Bible first. Yes, let us look at the headlines, but let us first study the Bible or else we run the danger of reading current events back into the Bible. As demonstrated, there exists a valid academic process that we can employ which uses scholarly sources and methodology, whereby we can objectively identify the various people groups depicted in Ezekiel 38:1–7. We have employed this method thus far in our study in order to ascertain the modern identity of Ezekiel's list of last-days invaders. Here are those we have identified thus far: *Put* is Libya, *Cush* is the Sudan, *Persia* is Iran, *Magog* is Central Asia, *Rosh* is Russia, and *Meshech, Tubal, Gomer* and *Togarmah* represent modern-day Turkey.

Biblical Places	Current Countries
Put	Libya
Cush	Sudan
Persia	Iran
Magog	Central Asia
Rosh	Russia
Meshech	Turkey
Tubal	Turkey
Gomer	Turkey
Togarmah	Turkey

ANCIENT NAMES, MODERN PLACES

RUSSIA
★ Rosh

KAZAKHSTAN
★ Magog

UZBEKISTAN
★ Magog

TURKMENISTAN
★ Magog

AFGHANISTAN
★ Magog

PAKISTAN
★ Magog

IRAN
★ Persia

UKRAINE
★ Magog

TURKEY
★ Mesech, Tubal, Gomer, Togarmah

ISRAEL

Caspian Sea

Black Sea

Mediterranean Sea

SUDAN
★ Cush

LIBYA
★ Put

CHAPTER

2

Considering the Psalm 83 War?

The end of Ezekiel 38:6 references, "many peoples with you." So Ezekiel's list of nations enumerated in Ezekiel 38:1–7 is not exhaustive. In other words, there could be other nations involved that Ezekiel does not specifically identify. Thus, the prophet appears to be merely highlighting some of the major players in the coming invasion rather than all of them. This realization of the non-exhaustive nature of Ezekiel's list becomes important since one of the views that has been popularized recently is the Psalm 83 War. The progenitor of this view, Bill Salus, has promoted it in his book called *Isralestine*.[16] Essentially, Salus

---

16 Bill Salus, *Isralestine: The Ancient Blueprints of the Future Middle East Policy* (Crane, MO: Anomalos, 2008). See also Bill Salus, *Psalm 83, the Missing Prophecy Revealed: How Israel Becomes the Next Mideast Superpower* (La Quinta, CA: Prophecy Depot, 2013).

argues that when you study Psalm 83 there is no mention of any of the names that Ezekiel mentions. Psalm 83 lists names of the nations or people groups that are closer or more adjacent to the land of Israel. Salus points out that Ezekiel 38 and 39 mentions nations that are farther removed.

Salus conjectures that the reason for this difference is due to the fact that there are actually going to be two different eschatological wars. First, there will be the Psalm 83 War in which Israel will emerge victorious, resulting in the increase of her national borders followed by a general time of political peace (Ezek. 38:8, 11). This time of peace will eventually be followed by the prophesied Gog and Magog War in which those nations mentioned in Ezekiel 38:1–7 will invade the nation of Israel. The supporting premise for the two end-time wars theory is that the invading nations mentioned in Psalm 83 are different from the nations mentioned in Ezekiel 38:1–7. However, they may not necessarily be different since Ezekiel 38:6 adds "many peoples with you." Therefore, if Psalm 83 is a prophecy about a future war, it is entirely possible that this war could occur concurrently or simultaneously with the Ezekiel 38 and 39 war rather than before and independent of it.

However, an even stronger argument exists that Psalm 83 is not a prophecy about a future war at all. It is more likely that Psalm 83 is merely an imprecatory Psalm where the Psalmist, in this case Asaph, is calling down judgment upon the perennial enemies of both God and Israel. Psalm 83 does not use the typical prophetic language that Ezekiel uses. Ezekiel routinely employs the phrase, "on that day" (Ezek. 38:10, 14; 39:11). By contrast, Psalm 83 fails to use similar prophetic language.

Beyond this, Chris White presents four reasons why Psalm 83 should not be interpreted as a prophetic war.[17]

First, the Psalm fails to describe any specific war or battle. Rather, it contains a record of Israel's enemies merely conspiring and conniving

---

17 See "The Psalm 83 'War' Debunked," <http://youtu.be/lCpDJootbO4>; Internet; accessed 27 May 2015. See also chapter 13, entitled "Problems with the Psalm 83 War," in Chris White, *False Christ: Will the Antichrist Claim to Be the Jewish Messiah?* (Ducktown, TN: CWM, 2014).

against her. Asaph's prayer in Psalm 83 is simply a petition that God will prevent these evil plans from ever materializing.

Second, as indicated above, the Psalm is devoid of prophetic language such as ". . . in the latter years you will. . . ." (Ezek. 38:8) and "At the end time. . . ." (Dan. 11:40) that is routinely found in other well-known Biblical prophecies.

Third, because all of the events and nations mentioned in Psalm 83 are consistent with the time of Asaph back in 950 B.C., there is no need to interpret this Psalm as an eschatological war. For example, it can be established that Ammon (2 Sam. 10:6) and Gebal (1 Kings 5:18) were active opponents of Israel in Asaph's day (Ps. 83:7).

Fourth, there are numerous other prayers in other Psalms that are quite similar to the prayer expressed in Psalm 83. Yet, these other prayers are obviously not prophecies. In other words, imprecatory prayers for God to intervene and destroy the nation's enemies, like the prayer expressed in Psalm 83, are replete throughout the Psalter (cf. Ps. 6:10; 7:6; 25:2, 19; 31:15; 56:2, 9; 69:18; 102:8). Yet most would not treat these similar prayers as some kind of predictive prophecy about a future war.

In addition, if there is going to be a future Psalm 83 War, then what about Psalm 2? If we interpret Psalm 2 in the same way that Salus interprets Psalm 83, then does Psalm 2 describe a future war also? In order to be consistent, we have to have a Psalm 2 War, a Psalm 83 War, then a Gog-Magog War. Thus, we see how ridiculous things rapidly become through a consistent application of Salus' interpretive methodology. Stanley Maughan, in his interview with Mark Hitchcock, quotes Hitchcock to this effect:

> Psalm 83 is kind of like Psalm 2, it is just saying that (there is similar language — why did the nations rage against Israel in Psalm 83) look there are people who are always against Israel. Israel is always going to have these enemies, they are always going to be against them and God is going to deal with them someday. We don't see a separate Psalm 2 war.[18]

---

18 Stanley A. Maughan, "Selected Expert Perspectives on Ezekiel 38–39 Related to Current World Events with Resulting Influence on Ministry Practices" (D.Min. diss., Dallas Theological Seminary, 2012), p. 257.

In sum, for the reasons stated, I do not believe that there is going to be a separate Psalm 83 War. Psalm 83 reads so differently from Ezekiel's prophecy that I do not take it to be a prophecy. However, even if it is a prophecy, the prophecy can be fulfilled concurrently with the Gog and Magog invasion rather than being independent and prior to it.

Now that we have answered the "Who?" question, let us move on to the "When?" question.

CHAPTER

3

When?

W
hen is this end-time invasion predicted by Ezekiel going to happen? There are at least seven views on the invasion's timing. The plethora of views on this topic indicates that it is a somewhat complicated matter. Thus, it becomes important for us to exercise patience on this issue as we seek truth. Most of these views emanate from Bible students within the traditional dispensationalist camp who are trying to wrestle with the text.

The reason for the complexity of the matter relates to the principle of progressive illumination related to prophetic Scripture. Daniel 12:4 says, "Conceal these words and seal up the book until the end of time; many will go back and forth, and knowledge will increase." A parallel passage is Amos 8:12:

> People will stagger from sea to sea
> And from the north even to the east;
> They will go to and fro to seek the word of the LORD,
> But they will not find it.

Going "back and forth" or "to and fro" relates to studying God's prophetic Word. As we get closer to the time period when these prophetic events will transpire, the prophetic scenario becomes progressively and gradually clearer and more understandable. As a point of clarity, there is no such thing as ongoing progressive revelation today. The Bible is complete. God has finished inspiring and recording the books of the Bible (cf. Jude 3; Rev. 22:18–19). However, there is a legitimate concept still in operation today called progressive illumination, whereby particularly the prophetic areas of Scripture become progressively clearer as we move ever closer to the time period when these events will unfold.

There are several other passages of Scripture that teach this notion of progressive illumination as it pertains to Biblical prophetic content. In 1 Peter 1:10–11, we read, "As to this salvation, the prophets who prophesied of the grace that *would come* to you made careful searches and inquiries, seeking to know what person or time the Spirit of Christ within them was indicating as He predicted the sufferings of Christ and the glories to follow."

Daniel 8:27 similarly says, "Then I, Daniel, was exhausted and sick for days. Then I got up *again* and carried on the king's business; but I was astounded at the vision, and there was none to explain *it*."

Interestingly, according to these verses, neither the Old Testament prophets nor Daniel himself back in the sixth century B.C. understood the full import of the prophecies that they had received from God. In fact, twice Daniel was specifically told that the meaning of the prophecies would not become clear until just before they were to come to pass. Daniel 12:4, as quoted above, states, "But as for you, Daniel, conceal these words and seal up the book until the end of time; many will go back and forth, and knowledge will increase." Daniel 12:9 similarly indicates, "Go *your way*, Daniel, for *these* words are concealed and sealed up until the end time." This principle of prophetic illumination helps us understand why a bewildering number of views have been generated as to the timing of the invasion. As we move closer to the time when the Gog and Magog

War will occur, the untenable views will begin to be more readily dismissed while the more tenable views will remain.

Let us turn our attention to examining seven views on the timing of the invasion. We will dispense with the least likely alternatives first and then proceed to the more probable options.

Esther 9

Gog and Magog War Prophesied by Ezekiel	Gog and Magog War Fulfilled
593 – 573 B.C.	483 – 473 B.C.

OLD TESTAMENT PERIOD	CHURCH AGE

The *first* view is the preterist view, which holds that Ezekiel's prophecy was fulfilled about a century after the time of the prophet Ezekiel in the events of Esther 9. A preterist is someone who believes that most, if not all, of Bible prophecy has already happened at some point in the past. In fact, the very word "preterist" means "past." R.C. Sproul, Hank Hanegraaff and Gary DeMar are examples of preterists. Although they are partial preterists in that they leave a few shreds of prophetic truth to be fulfilled in the future, by and large they believe that most of Bible prophecy has already been fulfilled in the remote past. They have written full-length books in defense of preterism. Hanegraaff's book is called *The Apocalypse Code*. Sproul's book is called *The Last Days According to Jesus*. DeMar's book is entitled *Last Days Madness*.[19] These interpreters are trying to argue that the Gog and Magog War of Ezekiel 38 and 39 already occurred in the book of Esther, chapter 9, back in 473 B.C.[20]

---

19 Hank Hanegraaff, *The Apocalypse Code* (Nashville, TN: Nelson, 2007); R. C. Sproul, *The Last Days According to Jesus* (Grand Rapids: Baker, 1998); Gary DeMar, *Last Days Madness*, 4th rev. ed. (Powder Springs, GA: American Vision, 1999).
20 Gary DeMar, *End Times Fiction: A Biblical Consideration of the Left Behind Theology* (Nashville, TN: Nelson, 2001), pp. 12–15.

Ancient Weapons?

Much of their argument develops from Ezekiel 38:4, where the prophet speaks of ancient weaponry: "horses and horsemen... buckler and shield." Preterists say these items could not be speaking of modern-day warfare. Because this verse is speaking of ancient warfare and weaponry, they believe that these chapters must be referring to a past event. However, it is possible for Ezekiel to be describing future warfare and weapons since he does not know how to speak of tanks and things of that nature. Instead, he simply uses words from his own sixth-century B.C. vocabulary. That could be why he is talking about ancient weapons, such as "horses and horsemen." After all, that is precisely what he is doing with mentioning all of these different ancient nations, as noted earlier. He does not refer to Iran or Turkey but rather to *Persia, Meshech,* etc. He uses language from his own day. It is also possible that he is following this same practice in his description of weaponry in Ezekiel 38:4.

Another possibility is that the ancient weapons depicted by Ezekiel are very literal. Consequently, the prophet is describing the exact kind of weaponry that will be used in this future battle. This view is espoused both by Dr. John F. Walvoord[21] and Dr. Paul Lee Tan.[22] According to this view, by the time these events happen—due to the peculiar circumstances of the day, such as depletion of the world's energy supply or disarmament agreements—there actually will be a return to ancient warfare practices. Thus, people will invade on horses and use ancient weaponry. Tan observes, "Interestingly, these prophesied military instruments though centuries old have not been made obsolete. The horse, for instance, is still used in warfare on certain kinds of terrain."[23] Ezekiel's description of ancient weaponry is an insufficient argument to justify pushing this whole prophecy back into the ancient past.

---

21   John F. Walvoord, *The Nations in Prophecy* (Grand Rapids: Zondervan, 1967), pp. 115–16.

22   Paul Lee Tan, *The Interpretation of Prophecy* (Winona Lake, IN: BMH, 1974), pp. 223–24.

23   Ibid., 223. See also Jon Ikin, "Downgrading for Armageddon: Does the Bible Suggest a Weapons Downgrade in the Last Days?," *Prophetic Witness,* March 2014, pp. 4–5.

Differences Between Ezekiel 38 and 39 & Esther 9

Beyond this, by comparing Ezekiel 38 and 39 to Esther 9, it becomes obvious that the two sections of Scripture are talking about two totally different and unrelated events.[24] In Ezekiel 38 and 39, Israel is invaded (38:16). In Esther 9, *Persia* is invaded (9:4). In Ezekiel 38 and 39, Israel is regenerated (39:22, 29). In Esther 9, Israel is never said to be regenerated. In Ezekiel 38 and 39, dead bodies are buried to cleanse Israel's land (39:12). In Esther 9, dead bodies are not buried in the land of Israel. In Ezekiel 38 and 39, the invaders are destroyed supernaturally (38:19–22). In Esther 9, the invaders are destroyed naturally (9:3–5). In Ezekiel 38 and 39, invaders come from the far west and north (38:5). In Esther 9, the invaders come from the near west and north (8:9). In Ezekiel 38 and 39, fire comes upon the invaders (39:6). In Esther 9, fire does not come upon the invaders. On and on we could go with these differences. Whatever the superficial points of similarity the two passages might share with one another, these are vastly outweighed by insurmountable differences separating the two. Thus, it is apparent that the events of Ezekiel 38 and 39 were not fulfilled in the events of Esther 9.

Futuristic Overall Context

It is difficult to connect this invasion with an event of past history. The reason for this difficulty, as will be explained below, is that these chapters comprise this futuristic section of Ezekiel's book (Ezek. 33–48). Consequently, the overall context of Ezekiel 38 and 39 awaits a future fulfillment just like everything else in Ezekiel's futuristic section. As Dyer notes, "Israel has been trampled underfoot by her enemies, but God will intervene in the future to insure her safety. He will defend His people and judge her enemies in distant countries (judgment on the nearby countries had already been cited, chaps. 25–32)."[25]

---

24   Mark Hitchcock and Thomas Ice, *The Truth Behind Left Behind* (Sisters: OR: Multnomah, 2004), p. 45.

25   Charles H. Dyer, "Ezekiel," in *The Bible Knowledge Commentary: An Exposition of the Scriptures by Dallas Seminary Faculty*, ed. John F. Walvoord and Roy B. Zuck (Colorado Springs, CO: Victor, 1985), p. 1,299.

Beginning of the Millennium

The *second* view places this war at the beginning of the millennial kingdom. Those who hold this view note that Ezekiel predicts that this war will take place while Israel is living at peace with her surrounding neighbors (Ezek. 38:8c, 11). The proponents further observe that Israel will finally be at peace with the surrounding nations once Jesus begins to rule and reign during the millennial age. Thus, this invasion must take place soon after the millennial kingdom begins. In other words, because it is a war that takes place during a time when Israel is at peace, the predicted invasion occurring during a time of peace describes the millennial kingdom, when Israel will be at peace. The big problem with this view is that in the millennial kingdom there will be no more war. Of the peaceful conditions during the millennial kingdom, Isaiah 2:4b says, "And they will hammer their swords into plowshares and their spears into pruning hooks. Nation will not lift up sword against nation, and never again will they learn war." The only war that will exist during this time period will be when Satan is released from his incarceration at the very end of the millennial kingdom so he can incite one final rebellion against God (Rev. 20:7–9). Until Satan is released, the millennial kingdom will be characterized by universal peace and rest. So, if this is true, how could Ezekiel's invasion transpire at the beginning of the millennial kingdom during a period when there will be no wars whatsoever and military peace is the norm? Walvoord explains:

> One of the hints given is that the battle takes place at a time when Israel has been re-gathered into their ancient land, and are dwelling securely and at rest. There are not too many times when Israel is it rest in God's prophetic program. . . . One point at which Israel will be at rest is in the millennial kingdom. But we are told expressly that, in the millennial

kingdom, there will be no war (Isaiah 2:4), and only when the rebellion occurs at the end of the millennium when Satan is let loose (Revelation 20:7–9) does war break out.[26]

Beyond this, the Millennium will only begin with believers (Matt. 25:31–46; John 3:3). If this is so, then where will the rebels come from who will invade Jerusalem at the beginning of the millennial kingdom? Dyer summarizes these aforementioned problems with the beginning-of-the-millennium view:

> Everyone who enters the Millennium will be a believer (John 3:3), and will have demonstrated his faith by protecting God's Chosen People (cf. comments on Matt. 25:31–46). At the beginning of the Millennium all weapons of war will be destroyed (Micah 4:1–4). Thus it seems difficult to see a war occurring when the unsaved warriors have been eliminated and their weapons destroyed.[27]

End of the Millennium

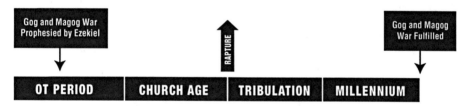

A *third* view is that this war will take place at the end of the millennial kingdom. They primarily get this notion from Revelation 20:8, which says, ". . . and will come out to deceive the nations which are in the four corners of the earth, Gog and Magog." Advocates of this view observe that these names, "Gog and Magog," mentioned in Revelation 20:8, are also the same names found in Ezekiel 38:2. Thus, they equate the events of Ezekiel 38 and 39 with the final satanic revolt that will take place at the end of the millennial kingdom (Rev. 20:7–9).

---

26 Walvoord, p. 114.
27 Dyer, p. 1,300.

Waterloo

It is most unlikely that the two prophetic passages are describing the same war. The reason that the names "Gog and Magog" are used in Revelation 20:8 is because the Ezekiel 38 and 39 War will become so famous after it occurs that by the time the end of the millennium rolls around, it will be only natural to analogize all wars to Ezekiel's Gog and Magog War of the past. This usage will be very similar to today's use of the term "Waterloo." Sometimes we hear people say, "I've met my Waterloo." In doing so, they are not saying that the Battle of Waterloo is literally being fought again. Rather, because Waterloo represented a great past conflict, it is used in the sense of a remembrance or a yardstick or a common way of depicting their own present conflict. In this sense, "Waterloo" becomes a figure of speech.

MacLeod well explains:

> How can Gog and Magog refer to a battle in Revelation 19 before the millennium and this battle at the end of the millennium? The most likely explanation is that Antichrist is Gog and will be defeated at the Second Coming. During the millennium his defeat will become a legend among the nations, something like Napoleon's defeat at Waterloo. Then at the end of the millennial kingdom the Gog and Magog "legend" is applied to a new historical situation (20:8), with Satan leading the new "Gog and Magog." Satan will meet his "Waterloo"—his "Gog and Magog."[28]

Differences Between Ezekiel 38 and 39 & Revelation 20:7–9

That Ezekiel 38 and 39 is an entirely different war from the one predicted in Revelation 20:7–9 becomes apparent by noting the many differences between the two passages.[29] Ezekiel 38 and 39 describe an invasion from specific nations—primarily coming from the north and west. Revelation 20:7–9 describes an invasion coming from all nations

---

28 David J. MacLeod, "The Fifth 'Last Thing': The Release of Satan and Man's Final Rebellion (Rev. 20:7–10)," *Bibliotheca Sacra* 157, no. 626 (April 2000): p. 209.

29 J. Dwight Pentecost, *Things to Come: A Study in Biblical Eschatology* (Findlay, OH: Dunham, 1958; reprint, Grand Rapids, Zondervan, 1964), pp. 349–50.

and directions. The Ezekiel 38 and 39 invasion chronologically flows into the millennial age (Ezek. 40–48). The war of Revelation 20:7–9 takes place after the millennial age has transpired. While the Ezekiel 38 and 39 invasion chronologically flows into the millennial age (Ezek. 40–48), the war of Revelation 20:7–9 chronologically flows into the eternal state (Rev. 21–22). After the Ezekiel 38 and 39 invasion, it will take seven months to dispose of the dead (Ezek. 39:12). The dead will be disposed of immediately following the war of Revelation 20:7–9 (Rev. 20:9). There is no record of the binding of Satan prior to the Ezekiel 38 and 39 invasion. However, Satan will have already been bound for an extended period of time prior to the events of Revelation 20:7–9. Also, "The effect on the people is different. In Ezekiel the battle is the catalyst God will use to draw Israel to Himself (cf. Ezek. 39:7, 22–29) and to end her captivity. But the battle in Revelation 20 will occur after Israel has been faithful to her God and has enjoyed His blessings for 1,000 years."[30]

In sum, the one superficial point of similarity—regarding the same name, "Gog and Magog"—allegedly uniting the two passages is vastly outweighed by insurmountable differences between the two.

Aftermath of the Invasion

One final problem with the end of the millennium view deserves attention. Ezekiel describes the aftermath of the battle to be a seven-month burying of the dead (Ezek. 39:12–13) and a seven-year burning of weapons (Ezek. 39:9–10). These cannot be events that will follow the final battle described in Revelation 20:7–9 since that battle will be chronologically followed by the resurrection of the unsaved and the Great White Throne Judgment(Rev. 20:11–15) as well as the eternal state (Rev. 21–22). It seems strange to drag the burying of the dead into a time when all unbelievers are being resurrected. It seems equally strange to have burning of weapons occurring during a time period when all things will be made new during the eternal state.

---

30 Dyer, p. 1,300.

Dyer summarizes:

> The results of Ezekiel's battle do not coincide with the events that follow the battle in Revelation 20. Why bury the dead for seven months after the battle (Ezek. 39:12–13) when the next prophetic event is the resurrection of the unsaved dead? (Rev. 20:11–13) Why would the people remain on earth after the battle to burn the weapons of war for seven years (Ezek. 39:9–10) instead of entering immediately into eternity? (Rev. 21:1–4) The events after each battle are so different that two separate battles must be assumed. . . . [31]

End of the Tribulation

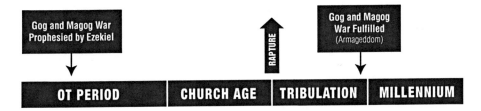

A *fourth* view is that Ezekiel's prophesied war is essentially the battle of Armageddon, which happens toward the end of the book of Revelation (Rev. 14:14–20; 16:13–16; 19:17–21). Again, as you go through Ezekiel 38 and 39 and compare it to the battle of Armageddon as described in Revelation, there are far more differences than similarities.[32] For example, Ezekiel 38 and 39 describe the invaders being instantaneously destroyed through convulsions of nature (Ezek. 38:20–22). Armageddon, on the other hand, seems to be more descriptive of a prolonged battle (Rev. 16:14, 16; 19:19). In Ezekiel 38 and 39, the invaders come from the far west and the north (Ezek. 38:5–6), but at Armageddon all nations—coming from all directions—will invade (Zech. 12:3; Rev. 16:14). In Ezekiel 38 and 39, the enemies are destroyed on Israel's mountains (Ezek. 39:2–4). At Armageddon the events will take place in the city of Jerusalem and in the valley of Jehoshaphat (Zech. 12:2; 14:2;

---

31 Ibid.
32 Pentecost, pp. 347–48.

Joel 3:2, 12). While at the time of the Ezekiel 38 and 39 invasion Israel seems to be dwelling in safety (Ezek. 38:8, 11), at Armageddon Israel will not be dwelling in safety (Rev. 12:14–17). In Ezekiel 38 and 39, no massive blood flow is recorded. At Armageddon, blood will flow as high as the horses' bridles for more than 200 miles (Rev. 14:20). In Ezekiel 38 and 39, the enemies will be destroyed by fire from heaven (Ezek. 39:6). No similar occurrence is found in Revelation's various Armageddon passages.

Before the Tribulation

A *fifth* view is that this war will happen before the great tribulation period even begins. Many of this view's advocates indicate that the war could happen before the rapture, but that it does not have to happen before the rapture. They argue in this manner since the moment one says something has to happen before the rapture, that is the moment one has damaged the imminency of the rapture. This doctrine of imminency teaches that the rapture is a signless event that could take place at any moment. In other words, there is no prophetic event that must happen before the rapture can occur. However, if one says the war *could* occur before the rapture, or that it could occur between the rapture and the beginning of the 70th week of Daniel, then they are not damaging the doctrine of imminency.

Others are more nuanced in articulating that the Ezekiel 38 and 39 War will be a post-rapture but pre-70th-week-of-Daniel event. Thomas Ice explains, "The next view, which is the one I hold at this time, is that it will happen after the rapture but before the tribulation.

It will be during the interval of days, weeks, months or years between the rapture and the start of the seven-year tribulation."[33]

Most prophecy charts that are drawn do not show a space of time between the rapture and the beginning of the tribulation period. Although we typically assume that these two events are going to happen in close proximity to one another, we really do not know that for sure. It is possible that there is a larger gap of time in between them. Consequently, many interpreters have placed Ezekiel's Gog–Magog War in this gap, including Tim LaHaye, Chuck Missler, Thomas Ice, Randall Price, Zola Levitt, Tom McCall, Mal Couch, Joel Rosenberg, Ron Rhodes, Stanely Maughan, David Cooper and Arnold Fruchtenbaum.

Burning of Weapons

Some have adopted this view on the grounds that Ezekiel 39:9–10 describes a seven-year burning of the weapons following the battle. They argue that if this battle begins at any point during the tribulation period then the burning of weapons must continue on into the millennium that will follow the tribulation period. For example, Fruchtenbaum writes, "*The middle of the Tribulation view* has problems with . . . the seven years. . . . The seven years would extend through the rest of the Tribulation and 3 and 1/2 years into the Millennium, making it inconsistent with the biblical view of the millennium."[34] Thus, by placing this battle before the tribulation begins, there is sufficient time to burn the weapons before the millennium starts.

Yet, why should we conclude that the burning of weapons following the battle cannot extend into any part of the millennial kingdom? After all, Babylon will perpetually burn throughout the millennial kingdom. Concerning Babylon's destruction, Revelation 19:1–3 predicts:

---

33 Thomas Ice, "Ezekiel 38 and 39 (Part 1)," <http://www.pre-trib.org/articles/view/ezekiel-38-39-part-1>; Internet; accessed 21 May 2015.

34 Arnold G. Fruchtenbaum, *Footsteps of the Messiah: A Study of the Sequence of Prophetic Events*, rev. ed. (Tustin, CA: Ariel, 2003), p. 122.

> After these things I heard something like a loud voice of a great multitude in heaven, saying, "Hallelujah! Salvation and glory and power belong to our God; BECAUSE HIS JUDGMENTS ARE TRUE AND RIGHTEOUS; for He has judged the great harlot who was corrupting the earth with her immorality, and HE HAS AVENGED THE BLOOD OF HIS BOND-SERVANTS ON HER." And a second time they said, "Hallelujah! HER SMOKE RISES UP FOREVER AND EVER."

If Babylon will be a burning reality throughout the duration of the millennium, since "her smoke" is said to arise "forever and ever," then why cannot the burning of weapons in the aftermath of Ezekiel's predicted war also burn right alongside Babylon during this same time period?

Invasion During Peace?

The major problem with the pre-tribulation view is that Ezekiel describes this war happening during a time of peace for the Jewish nation. This peace is described in Ezekiel 38:8 and 11.

Ezekiel 38:8 states, "After many days you will be summoned; in the latter years you will come into the land that is restored from the sword, *whose inhabitants* have been gathered from many nations to the mountains of Israel which had been a continual waste; but its people were brought out from the nations, and they are living securely, all of them." Ezekiel 38:11 continues, "And you will say, 'I will go up against the land of unwalled villages. I will go against those who are at rest, that live securely, all of them living without walls and having no bars or gates.'"

Advocates of this position will counter by saying that the peace and "unwalled villages" mentioned in these verses only refer to security. They will then note how secure the modern state of Israel is. After all, she has successfully repelled all of the overwhelming modern attacks aimed against her, such as those launched in 1948, 1967, 1973 and so forth. As Fruchtenbaum explains:

> This is not a security due to a state of peace, but a security due to confidence in their own strength. This, too, is a good description of Israel today. The Israeli army has fought four major wars since its founding and won

them swiftly each time. Today Israel is secure, confident that her army can repel any invasion from the Arab states. Hence, Israel is dwelling securely. Israel is dwelling in unwalled villages (Ezek. 38:11).[35]

However, the view begins to break down upon realizing that in Ezekiel 38:11 there is not just one word describing Israel's condition at the time of the invasion, but rather two Hebrew words. One of those words (*batach*), translated "unwalled villages," refers to security. However, there is a totally different word also used in Ezekiel 38:11. It is the word (*shacat*) translated "at rest." *BDB* says that this word speaks of a state of tranquility or being "quiet, undisturbed."[36] It is difficult to see Israel in that condition today, given what we see consistently happening to Israel on the news as she endures perpetual terrorist attacks and suicide bombings and continues in a survival mode as a tiny nation in the midst of hostile Islamic dictatorships perpetually threatening to wipe her off the map. As Hitchcock explains:

> It is true that the inhabitants of modern Israel live in unwalled villages and have some degree of security due to their military might. However, they are not "at rest" as required by Ezek 38:11. The Hebrew word translated "at rest" means "be quiet, undisturbed." This hardly describes Israel today. The nation is one huge armed camp. The people are disturbed on a regular basis by threats and homicide bombings. Since 1948, Israel has lived under the constant threat of terrorist attacks and invasion by her neighbors. The terminology in Ezek 38 fits much better with the first half of the seventieth week of Daniel when Israel will enjoy the protection of her covenant with Antichrist and will temporarily let down her guard (Dan 9:27).[37]

Walvoord concurs when he writes:

> One of the principal questions one could ask about this battle is, When is the battle going to occur? . . . Unfortunately, varying opinions have been offered by capable Bible scholars on this point, and there has been considerable disagreement. . . . It will not be possible to consider all these views in detail, but there are some hints that provide a good clue as to when this battle will take place. One of the hints given is that the battle takes place at a time when Israel has been regathered into their ancient land,

---

35 Ibid., pp. 121–22.
36 Brown, Driver and Briggs, eds., pp. 1,052–53.
37 Hitchcock, "The Battle of Gog and Magog," pp. 14–15.

and is dwelling securely and at rest. There are not too many times when Israel is at rest in God's prophetic program. They have been scattered and persecuted over the face of the earth, and not even in the future will Israel have many periods of rest. Certainly, Israel is not at rest today. Israel is an armed camp, living under a truce with their Arab neighbors about them. Their enemies would drive every Israelite into the Mediterranean Sea and kill them if they could. . . . There is only one period in the future that clearly fits this description of Ezekiel, and this is the first half of Daniel's seventieth week of God's program for Israel (Daniel 9:27).[38]

End of Tribulation Events

Beyond this problem of the invasion transpiring during a time of Israel's peace, the pretribulation view also suffers further problems since much of the language of Ezekiel's prophecy relates far better to the end of the tribulation rather than before the tribulation period even begins. Advocates of the pretribulational timing of Ezekiel 38 and 39 are not just contending that part of the prophecy will take place before the tribulation period begins. Rather, they are arguing that all of the prophecy, both the invasion and the Divine destruction of the invaders, will all be accomplished before the tribulation period even begins.

Rhodes notes:

> Once God destroys Russia and the Muslim invaders prior to the tribulation, the Antichrist would be free to rise as the leader of the revived Roman Empire—a European superstate. . . . If God destroys the Muslim invaders prior to the beginning of the tribulation, the antichrist could more easily sign a peace pact with Israel (Daniel 9:27), guaranteeing that Israel will be protected. In other words, Israel will be easier to protect if the Muslim forces are already out of the picture. . . . This scenario, like the previous one, may account for Israel's ability to construct the Jewish temple on the temple mount in Jerusalem. With Muslim forces destroyed, Muslim resistance will be greatly minimized.[39]

Ice similarly observes:

---

38 Walvoord, pp. 113–15.
39 Ron Rhodes, *Northern Storm Rising: Russia, Iran, and the Emerging End-Times Military Coalition against Israel* (Eugene, OR: Harvest, 2008), pp. 182–83.

The next view, which is the one I hold at this time, is that it will happen after the rapture but before the tribulation. It will be during the interval of days, weeks, months or years between the rapture and the start of the seven-year tribulation. This view also accounts for the seven years of Ezekiel 39:9. I have always thought that one of the strengths of this view is the way in which it could set the stage for the Biblical scenario of the tribulation. If the tribulation is closely preceded by a failed regional invasion of Israel, in other words Russia and her Muslim allies, then this would remove much of the Russian and Muslim influence currently in the world today and allow a Euro-centric orientation to arise. So the tribulation is preceded by a failed regional attack on Israel and this is why the tribulation ends with all the peoples of the world attacking Israel at Armageddon. It could also set the stage for the rebuilding of the Temple as a result of Islamic humiliation.[40]

Yet, much of the language of pertaining to the aftermath of the Ezekiel 38 and 39 invasion relates to the end of the tribulation rather than before it starts. Once this battle ends, Ezekiel 39:4 and 39:17–18 both speak of beasts and birds feasting on the carnage of all of the dead bodies.

Ezekiel 39:4 foretells, "You will fall on the mountains of Israel, you and all your troops and the peoples who are with you; I will give you as food to every kind of predatory bird and beast of the field."

Ezekiel 39:17 similarly states, "And as for you, son of man, thus says the Lord God, 'Speak to every kind of bird and to every beast of the field, "Assemble and come, gather from every side to My sacrifice which I am going to sacrifice for you, as a great sacrifice on the mountains of Israel, that you may eat flesh and drink blood.""

According to Matthew 24:27–29 and Revelation 19:17–18, such carnage feasting is something that happens at the end of the tribulation period, and not before it.

Matthew 24:27–29 states,

For just as the lightning comes from the east and flashes even to the west, so will the coming of the Son of Man be. Wherever the corpse is, there the vultures will gather. But immediately after the tribulation of those days THE SUN WILL BE DARKENED, AND THE MOON WILL

40 Thomas Ice, "Ezekiel 38 and 39 (Part 1)," <http://www.pre-trib.org/articles/view/ezekiel-38-39-part-1>; Internet; accessed 21 May 2015.

NOT GIVE ITS LIGHT, AND THE STARS WILL FALL from the sky, and the powers of the heavens will be shaken.

Matthew connects this carnage feasting with the events of the great tribulation during the second half of Daniel's 70th week (Matt. 24:15, 21–22) and the second advent (Matt. 24:27, 30) that will occur at the end of the week. Revelation 19:17–18 similarly explains,

> Then I saw an angel standing in the sun, and he cried out with a loud voice, saying to all the birds which fly in midheaven, "Come, assemble for the great supper of God, so that you may eat the flesh of kings and the flesh of commanders and the flesh of mighty men and the flesh of horses and of those who sit on them and the flesh of all men, both free men and slaves, and small and great."

Notice that John also portrays such carnage feasting as something that will chronologically follow Christ's second advent (cf. Rev. 19:11–16) at the end of the tribulation period.

In addition to carnage feasting, Ezekiel also describes Israel's national regeneration as a consequence and aftermath of this invasion. Dyer explains: "In Ezekiel the battle is the catalyst God will use to draw Israel to Himself."[41] He further observes, "The ultimate result in the battle with Gog will be Israel's national repentance and spiritual restoration. This will be fulfilled in the millennial kingdom."[42] Ezekiel 39:22 describes the spiritual impact that this invasion will have on national Israel when it says, "And the house of Israel will know that I am the LORD their God from that day onward." Ezekiel 39:29 similarly states, "'I will have poured out My Spirit on the house of Israel,' declares the Lord GOD." In other words, the aftermath of this war is a converted Israel.

> The aftermath of this war is a converted Israel.

---

41 Dyer, p. 1,300.
42 Ibid., p. 1,302.

The problem with the pre-tribulation timing view of Ezekiel 38 and 39 is that if you place the whole battle and its consequences between the rapture and the beginning of the 70th week of Daniel, you will discover a converted Israel before the tribulation period even starts. Now it seems strange to think that Israel will be converted before the tribulation period ever begins. The very purpose of the tribulation period is to convert Israel (cf. Dan. 9:24). Jeremiah 30:7 describes this purpose, "Alas! for that day is great, There is none like it; And it is the time of Jacob's distress, But he will be saved from it." Simply put, why would Israel be converted before the tribulation period begins when Bible prophecy consistently predicts that God will use this very tribulation period to convert Israel? This seems to pose a chronological problem for the pre-tribulational view.

Pre-tribulational invasion advocate Stanley Maughan seems to recognize this chronological problem. Consequently, in order to sustain his view, he marginalizes the notion that verses Ezekiel 39:22 and 29 are speaking of a national Israeli conversion. He states:

> While certainly one outcome of this war will be the salvation of many Jews, it does not require the wholesale conversion of all Jews . . . . It is better to understand this as a recognition among all that God is at work, without necessarily experiencing a genuine conversion . . . . Nevertheless, God will use the dramatic events of this war to help bring many Jews to faith, whether in the immediate aftermath, or in conjunction with other events during the period of the Great Tribulation.[43]

However, Maughan dramatically understates the full import of these verses. Concerning their true meaning, the comments of Charles Lee Feinberg are far more on target:

> Verses 25–29 teach that the *complete* return of Israel will occur after the defeat of Gog and his Confederates. Ezekiel summarized his prophecies of hope and restoration. When he stated that God will have mercy upon the whole house of Israel, he had in mind that all previous restorations were partial. Now a *universal and final restoration* will take place. It was God who allowed them to go into captivity; it is he who will see

---

43 Maughan, p. 107.

to it that they are regathered; indeed, it is he who will insure that *not one is left out of the land.* . . . In conclusion, to summarize all the benefits promised, Ezekiel spoke of the outpouring of the Spirit upon the house of Israel (italics added).[44]

First Half of the Tribulation

The *sixth* view on the timing of Ezekiel 38 and 39 is that this invasion will take place in the first half of the tribulation. This view seems closer to what Ezekiel predicts than any of the other timing views discussed thus far.

Timing Clues

There are *five* timing clues in Ezekiel's prophecy that lead us to this conclusion.

First, this war is in the restoration section of the book of Ezekiel. The book of Ezekiel has three parts. Chapters 1–24 are judgments to imminently come upon Judah. Chapters 25–32 are judgments to imminently come upon the nations surrounding Judah. Chapters 33–48 represent the future restoration of the nation of Israel. Chapters 1–24 are symmetrical to chapters 33–48, counterbalanced by that fulcrum in the middle which is Ezekiel's prediction of judgment upon the surrounding nations (25–32). In the first section Ezekiel is commissioned, and in the last section he is recommissioned. In the first section he is commissioned to preach judgment, and in the last section he is commissioned to preach restoration. In the first section his mouth is closed, and in the last section his mouth

---

44 Charles L. Feinberg, *The Prophecy of Ezekiel: The Glory of the Lord*, paperback ed. (Chicago: Moody, 1969; reprint, Chicago: Moody, 1984), pp. 231–32.

is opened. In the first section the glory of God departs from the temple, and in the last section the glory of God returns to the temple.[45] The Gog and Magog war is in that third major section of the book of Ezekiel, with all of the other eschatological material, such as the millennial temple (Ezek. 40–46), the division of the tribal territories among the various tribes during the millennium (Ezek. 47–48), the valley of the dry bones (Ezek. 37) and the great eschatological political and spiritual regathering of the nation (Ezek. 36). Thus, the aforementioned preterist view could not be correct. This is not a war that has already happened. Rather, this is a war yet to come since it is mentioned along with the other eschatological events in Ezekiel's book.

A *second* clue is the reference to "the latter years" in Ezekiel 38:8.

The *third* clue is the reference to "the last days" in Ezekiel 38:16. When you study *last days*, not in the Pauline epistles, but rather in the prophets, *last days* refers to Israel's end-time discipline and future kingdom (cf. Isa. 2:2; Jer. 23:29; 30:24; Hos. 3:5; Mic. 4:1).[46] We have to keep Biblical uses of the expression *last days* distinct based upon context. *Last days* does not mean the same thing everywhere and every time the phrase is employed in Scripture. In other words, the expression *last days* should not be misunderstood as a technical term. When Paul talks about "the last days," as "in the last days difficult times will come" (2 Tim. 3:1), he is talking about the last days of the church. As a dispensationalist, I see God working different programs—one for the church and one for Israel. Sometimes *last days* refers to the church and sometimes this phrase refers to Israel. So it is very important that we define *last days* based upon the context. Ezekiel here is speaking about Israel's last days.

A *fourth* clue is that this war will take place after Israel's regathering in unbelief, but before Israel is restored spiritually. Ezekiel 38:8 states, "After many days you will be summoned; in the latter years you will come into the land that is restored from the sword, *whose inhabitants* have been gathered from many nations to the mountains of Israel which had been

---

45 Dyer, p. 1,226.
46 Hitchcock, "*The Battle of Gog and Magog*," p. 13.

a continual waste; but its people were brought out from the nations, and they are living securely, all of them." What is being described here is Israel being regathered in a state of unbelief. However, by the time this war ends, Israel will be in faith (Ezek. 39:22, 29). Ezekiel 39:22 states, "And the house of Israel will know that I am the LORD their God from that day onward." Ezekiel 39:29 says, "'I will not hide My face from them any longer, for I will have poured out My Spirit on the house of Israel,' declares the Lord GOD."

The Bible predicts two eschatological regatherings for national Israel. There is first a present regathering in unbelief when Israel returns to part of the land. This regathering will be followed by another future regathering when Israel will return to all of the land in faith. In this current regathering she is restored to part of the land. In the final regathering she will be restored to all of the land. The current regathering is a restoration to the land only. The second regathering will be a restoration to both the land and the Lord. The current regathering of the Jews that we are now seeing is setting the stage for discipline during the tribulation period. The latter regathering will be after Israel is saved or regenerated and it will set the stage for the millennial kingdom.[47] Ezekiel's Gog and Magog war will take place between those two regatherings. Ezekiel clearly places this war after Israel has been regathered in unbelief (Ezek. 38:8) before she is spiritually restored (Ezek. 39:22, 29). This first regathering started when the Jewish state declared her independence in 1948. Thus, the Ezekiel 38 and 39 war has to happen sometime between 1948 and Israel's ultimate restoration during the tribulation period.

The *fifth* timing clue regarding when this war will happen is that Israel will be living in both security and peace. As mentioned earlier, in Ezekiel 38:11, there are two words used to describe Ezekiel's position just prior to the invasion: "And you will say, 'I will go up against the land of unwalled villages. I will go against those who are at *rest*, that live *securely*, all of them living without walls and having no bars or gates'" (italics added). Thus, this verse is not merely speaking of security but also of Israel living in a condition where

---

47 J. Randall Price, *Jerusalem in Bible Prophecy: God's Stage for the Final Drama* (Eugene, OR: Harvest House, 1998), p. 219.

she is quiet, undisturbed, restful and peaceful. There are only *two* times in her history when such security and tranquility will be possible.[48] *One* era will be during the millennial kingdom (Isa. 2:4). However, this war cannot take place during the millennial kingdom because, as explained earlier, there will be no more war during the millennium (Mic. 4:3–4).

The only *other time* it could be possible for the existence of Israel's national peace will be when the Antichrist comes to power and enters into a peace treaty with national Israel, thereby guaranteeing her protection and survival. That is the very event that will begin the seven-year countdown leading to Christ's second advent, according to Daniel 9:27. This will be during a time when the nations will be saying "peace and safety," but then "destruction will" quickly come (1 Thess. 5:3; cf. Rev. 6:1–4). Thus, this invasion will take place during this time after the Antichrist has come to power and guarantees Israel's survival. Dyer well explains:

> It seems best to place Ezekiel's battle of Gog and Magog in the Tribulation period. Other internal markers indicate that it should be placed in the first three and one-half years of the seven-year period. The attack will come when Israel is at peace (Ezek. 38:8, 11). When Israel's covenant with the Antichrist is in effect at the beginning of Daniel's 70th Week (Dan. 9:27a), she will be at peace. But after the covenant is broken at the middle of the seven-year period, the nation will suffer tremendous persecution (Dan. 9:27b; Matt. 24:15–22). This will provide the time needed to bury the dead (Ezek. 39:12–13) and to burn the weapons of war (39:9–10). So the battle described by Ezekiel may take place sometime during the first three and one-half years of the seven-year period before Christ's second coming.[49]

Walvoord also notes:

> There is only one period in the future that clearly fits this description of Ezekiel, and that is the first half of Daniel's seventieth week of God's program for Israel (Daniel 9:27) . . . . He will enter into a seven-year covenant of protection and peace with the people of Israel (Daniel 9:27). Under that covenant, Israel will be able to relax, for their Gentile enemies will have become their friends, apparently guaranteeing their borders and

---

48 Mark Hitchcock, *Middle East Burning: Is the Spreading Unrest a Sign of the Times?* (Eugene, OR: Harvest House, 2012), p. 81; Walvoord, pp. 114–15.

49 Dyer, p. 1,300.

promised them freedom. During that first three and one-half years, we have the one time when regathered Israel is at rest and secure. Apparently Russia will invade the land of Israel during that period, possibly toward its close, and the Scripture will then be fulfilled.[50]

Notice that Ezekiel describes Israel moving from peace (Ezek. 38:8, 11) to war (Ezek. 38:9, 12). When we harmonize this transition with the book of Revelation, it is a perfect description of the first two seal judgments. The breaking of the first seal will bring forth the rider on the white horse or the Antichrist. He will come forward and usher in momentary peace (Rev. 6:1–2). However, during the second seal judgment warfare will break out (Rev. 6:3–4). Thus, I believe that Ezekiel's Gog and Magog war will take place beginning with the second seal judgment as depicted in the book of Revelation. In other words, the ambition to invade Israel in the minds of the hostile nations will begin to manifest itself while the first seal is in effect. However, the actual invasion itself will terminate this first seal judgment and introduce the warfare spoken of in the second seal judgment. Placing the invasion toward the beginning of the tribulation period in this manner is the traditional Dallas Theological Seminary view as taught by J. Dwight Pentecost, John F. Walvoord and Charles C. Ryrie.

Problems with the View

While the first half of the tribulation view is closer to the truth than the previously described views, it contains a significant deficiency giving rise to the necessity of a seventh and slightly more nuanced view. A problem with this view emerges if you completely place all of the contents of Ezekiel's prophecy into events surrounding the second seal judgment. As mentioned earlier, Ezekiel 39 contains prophetic language that only fits the end of the tribulation period. So, where do you place Israel's conversion (Ezek. 39:22, 29) when other prophetic Scripture seems to indicate that such a national conversion will transpire at the end of the tribulation period, thereby triggering Christ's second advent(Matt. 23:37–39)? But timewise, where do you place the birds and the beasts

---

50 Walvoord, p. 115.

feasting on the carnage (Ezek. 39:4, 17–18)? As mentioned earlier, this seems to be an event which happens at the end of the tribulation period (Matt. 24:27–28; Rev. 19:17–18).

Two-Phase View

Gog and Magog War Prophesied by Ezekiel	RAPTURE	Gog and Magog Prophecy	
		Ezekiel 38	Ezekiel 39

OT PERIOD	CHURCH AGE	TRIBULATION	MILLENNIUM
		3.5 Years 3.5 Years	

The *seventh* and best view is known as the two-phase view. Simply put, this view contends that Ezekiel 38 happens towards the beginning of the tribulation period as described in view six. However, view six errs in assuming that Ezekiel 39 is also tied to events related to the first-half of the tribulation period. Ezekiel 39 is not about events toward the beginning of the tribulation period. Rather, the chapter is about the end of the tribulation period. In other words, Ezekiel 38 transpires commensurate with the second seal judgment as noted earlier. Moreover, Ezekiel 39 is not speaking of the initial invasion but rather its aftermath and lingering effects existing after most of the tribulation period has run its course. I was never even aware of this view until one of my professors, Harold Hoehner, expressed it in a book entitled *Essays in Honor of Donald Campbell*.[51] Thus, the two chapters in Ezekiel 38 and 39 are portrayed as more of a process rather than as a singular prophecy, with both of them being fulfilled at roughly the same time.

This observation should come as no great surprise to careful students of the book of Ezekiel since the prophet often describes eschatological events as parts of a prolonged process. For example, in Ezekiel's vision of

---

51 Harold W. Hoehner, *"The Progression of Events in Ezekiel 38–39,"* in *Integrity of Heart, Skillulness of Hands: Biblical and Leadership Studies in Honor of Donald K. Campbell,* ed. Charles H. Dyer and Roy B. Zuck (Grand Rapids: Baker, 1994), pp. 82–92.

the valley of dry bones (Ezek. 37:1–14), the prophet describes the bones assembling, the flesh appearing on the bones and finally the breath of life entering this newly formed body. Most would not understand this as being fulfilled in a singular prophetic event. Rather, it is likely a prophecy involving a prolonged process.

First, Israel is returned to her homeland beginning in 1948. Then, she will experience a time of discipline known as the great tribulation. Through such discipline, she will come to know Christ and will consequently be regenerated leading to the millennial age. So in Ezekiel 37:11–14, Ezekiel foresaw a singular prophecy spanning arguably several decades. The same prolonged process is also in view in the prior chapter (Ezek. 36:24–28). Ezekiel 36:24 describes the Jews first being regathered back to their "own land." Then the prophet narrates Israel's spiritual regeneration (Ezek. 36:25–28) as a result of the tribulation period. Notice, once again, Ezekiel is making reference to a process arguably beginning in 1948 and then spanning several decades.

Thus, an interpretation of Ezekiel 38 and 39 that sees chapter 38 as the beginning of the process and chapter 39 as the end of the same process is in harmony with how Ezekiel recorded his other eschatological visions. Most of the other aforementioned interpretations of these chapters seem to prematurely and falsely presuppose that both Ezekiel 38 and Ezekiel 39 are speaking of a singular event. Yet, as has been demonstrated, such a presupposition may be inaccurate. In sum, putting chapter 38 at the beginning of the tribulation period and chapter 39 toward the end is the best explanation that I have heard on this difficult and somewhat controversial timing issue thus far, thus answering the "When?" question.

CHAPTER

4

Why?

N ow let's move on to the "Why?" question. Why is this war going to happen and what will be the motivation of those doing the invading? Ezekiel reveals *two* motivations of those attacking Israel in the last days.

Anti-Semitism

The *first* motivation will be anti-Semitism. Ezekiel 38:10 prophesies, "Thus says the Lord GOD, 'It will come about on that day, that thoughts will come into your mind and you will devise an evil plan.'" Consequently, verse 16 says, "And you will come up against My people Israel."

Who is it that puts evil thoughts into people's minds? It is the devil, of course. For example, David had a desire to number the troops of Israel and 1 Chronicles 21:1 tells us that Satan put that very idea into David's mind. Peter's mind, too, was also infiltrated by a satanic thought.

Peter had an idea that he had to talk Jesus Christ out of dying on the cross.

> Peter took Him aside and began to rebuke Him, saying, "God forbid *it*, Lord! This shall never happen to You." But He turned and said to Peter, "Get behind Me, Satan! You are a stumbling block to Me; for you are not setting your mind on God's interests, but man's" (Matt. 16:22-23).

In a similar way, according to Ezekiel 38:10, at some future point "thoughts will come into" the minds of these hostile nations. Thus, they will say now is the time to take Israel down. Why would Satan put such thoughts into the minds of these leaders? Satan hates the nation of Israel with a passion. The reason for this animosity relates to what God said back in Genesis 12:2–3 to Abraham and his physical descendants:

> And I will make you a great nation,
> And I will bless you,
> And make your name great;
> And so you shall be a blessing;
> And I will bless those who bless you,
> And the one who curses you I will curse.
> And in you all the families of the earth will be blessed.

Consequently, every spiritual blessing that we currently enjoy has come to us through the nation of Israel.

For example, the Scriptures have come to us through the Jewish people (cf. Rom. 3:2). Jesus Christ the Messiah and Savior was a Jew (cf. John 4:22; Rom. 9:5). However, there is yet a third blessing on the horizon. God has not finished blessing the world through Israel. In this sense, Israel is "the gift that keeps on giving." This third blessing that is yet to come will be the kingdom. This coming kingdom will not be headquartered in Washington, D. C., New York, Brussels or any other Gentile city. Rather, the coming kingdom will be headquartered in the city of Jerusalem (cf. Isa. 2:2–3; Zech. 14:16–18; Rev. 20:9). The day is coming when Christ will govern the entire world from the city of Jerusalem. During this glorious kingdom age, Satan will be bound for 1,000 years in a place of temporary incarceration called "the abyss" (Rev. 20:2–3).

At the conclusion of Christ's earthly kingdom, Satan will be permanently "thrown into the lake of fire" (Rev. 20:10). Satan works preemptively in history in an attempt to prevent God's promises from ever coming to pass (Rev. 12:1–5). Satan has always wanted to take out Israel prematurely so that these blessings cannot unfold (Rev. 12:6–17). Apparently, he will make one last grand and final attempt by prompting the surrounding nations to attack and eradicate Israel from the earth so that Christ's second coming (Matt. 23:38–39), the subsequent kingdom and his own dethronement from over the earth can be prevented.

Wealth

The *second* reason for this attack has to do with wealth or money. "Follow the money," as people often say. Ezekiel 38:12 provides the motive of these attackers, "To capture spoil and to seize plunder, to turn your hand against the waste places which are *now* inhabited, and against the people who are gathered from the nations, who have acquired cattle and goods, who live at the center of the world." Thus, the motive of this attack is money.

REASONS FOR THE WAR

1 - *Anti-Semitism*   2 - *Wealth*

It remains an indisputable fact that ever since Israel got her territory back in 1948 and gained even more territory in 1967, Israel's gross domestic product has outstripped that of her surrounding neighbors. According to Matthew Kreiger recently in the *Jerusalem Post*:

> Despite a population of only slightly more than 7 million people . . . Israel is now home to more than 7,200 millionaires . . . . Of the 500 wealthiest people in the world, six are now Israeli, and all told, Israel's rich had assets in 2007 of more than $35 billion dollars . . . . Israel's GDP is almost double that of any other Middle Eastern country. [52]

When the Arabs controlled that part of the world, the land was destitute and lacked agricultural and economic viability. For example, in 1867, Mark Twain visited Israel. He wrote about his experiences in his book *Innocents Abroad*. In this book, he hardly describes the vibrant and prosperous Israel of today, but rather a desolate country that was devoid of both vegetation and human population. He observed:

> . . . A desolate country whose soil is rich enough, but is given over wholly to weeds . . . a silent mournful expanse . . . a desolation is here that not even imagination can grace with the pomp of life and action . . . we never saw a human being on the whole route . . . there was hardly a tree or shrub anywhere. Even the olive tree and the cactus, those fast friends of a worthless soil, had almost deserted the country.[53]

However, after Israel gained control of this area, that land became a flourishing agricultural center. Consequently, there exists a deep-seated animosity and jealousy in these surrounding nations because of this Israeli-influenced economic turnaround.

Today, Israel appears to be on the verge of accumulating even more wealth. According to one source:

> The value of the minerals of the Dead Sea is estimated at five trillion dollars. This estimate appears to be optimistic but it is supported in part by the report of the Crown Agents of the British Colonies entitled "Production

---

52 As cited in David Jeremiah, *What in the World Is Going On? 10 Prophetic Clues You Cannot Afford to Ignore* (Nashville: Nelson, 2008), p. 175.

53 Mark Twain, *The Innocents Abroad, Complete*, 1st ed. (A Public Domain Book, 1869), pp. 267, 285 and 302. These quotes can be found in chapters 47, 49 and 52.

of Minerals From the Waters of the Dead Sea".... This official report estimates the minerals, except oil, in 1925 as follows: Magnesium Chloride, 22,000 tons, value 600 billion dollars; Potassium Chloride, 20,000 tons, value 75 billion dollars; other minerals valued at 1,200 billion dollars; or a total of about three trillion dollars, exclusive of oil.[54]

In the summer of 2010, "... huge deposits of natural gas were found along Israel's northern coastline."[55] Others have speculated that Israel may be on the precipice of a vast discovery of oil.

> Israel is actually sitting on top of a vast amount of oil. According to Harold Vinegar, the former chief scientist of Royal Dutch Shell, the Shefla Basin holds the world's second-largest shale deposits outside the United States, from which around 250 billion barrels of oil—about the same as Saudi Arabia's proven reserves. The basin is located a few miles south of Tel Aviv. We've known about oil shale for several decades. There is a huge amount of oil in shale. Estimates of global deposits range from 2.8 trillion to 3.3 trillion barrels of recoverable oil. The problem is getting the oil out of the sedimentary material. You can't just drill a well and pump out the oil. It's like trying to squeeze water out of a frozen sponge. As our technology improves, we are able to extract oil from fields that were once beyond our reach. A few decades ago, we had no way of getting crude from the ocean. Now, we can drill in water that is several miles deep. The technology curb has now reached the point where shale is becoming an exploitable resource. We currently use a fracking technique to remove gas from shale, and oil may be next. Oil-shale mining used to be a dirty business that used up tremendous amounts of water and energy. New technology will use heating units to separate the oil from the shale safely and at low cost. Israel Energy Initiatives estimates the marginal cost of production at between $35 and $40 per barrel.... The odds are long against shale oil, but Israel is probably the best to make it work. Unlike most deposits, the Shefla shale is in a hospitable location. It also contains oil of the light, sweet variety that is easy to refine into gasoline or other common end products. Most of all, the Jews have proven themselves to be very talented at exploiting resources. If they can't make shale oil work, I doubt any nation can.[56]

---

54 <http://www.matterofprinciple.net/011/11/rothschilds-palestine.html>; Internet; accessed 15 December 2011. Although there is a wide variation of estimates, many different sources estimate the mineral wealth of the Dead Sea in the trillions of dollars.

55 Todd Strandberg, "Could Israel Become a Major Oil Exporter," <www.bibleprophecy.com>; Internet; accessed 26 May 2015.

56 Ibid.

Walvoord similarly notes:

> Progress in agriculture and reclamation of the land has been matched to some extent by establishment of industries. Textiles have now become an important part of Israel's production. The cutting of diamonds imported for this purpose, the manufacture of military weapons and arms, and the exploitation of the measureless chemical wealth of the Dead Sea are major factors of Israel's economy. Some oil has already been discovered as well as gas. One by one problems that beset Israel at the beginning are being solved.[57]

Thus, Rhodes conjectures, "A recent and unexpected major oil discovery may be among the motivating factors for the future Ezekiel invasion."[58] In fact, in recent days, the conversation regarding a discovery of oil in Israel has transitioned from one of mere speculation to rather one of an accomplished reality.

> After more than a year of round-the-clock drilling, large amounts of oil have been found on the Golan Heights. Estimates are that the amount of oil discovered will make Israel self-sufficient for very many years to come. Afek Oil and Gas chief geologist Dr. Yuval Bartov told Channel 2 News, "We are talking about a strata which is 350 meters thick and what is important is the thickness and the porosity. On average in the world strata are 20-30 meters thick, so this is ten times as large as that, so we are talking about significant quantities. The important thing is to know the oil is in the rock and that's what we now know." Three drillings have so far taken place in the southern Golan Heights which have found large reserves of oil. Potential production is dramatic - billions of barrels, which will easily provide all Israel's oil needs. Israel consumes 270,000 barrels of oil per day. Although the existence of the oil in the ground is a fact, the critical phase now is to check how easily it can be extracted and whether it involves high production costs. In a period of very low oil prices, extraction will have to be relatively cheap to make exploitation of the field profitable. Just as Israel's offshore Mediterranean gas discoveries have created an entire energy industry, so the Golan oil find could also generate a new industry around it. But while the gas has been found dozens of kilometers from Israel, the Golan find is much closer. . . . Bartov said, "There is enormous excitement.

---

57 John F. Walvoord, *Israel in Prophecy* (Grand Rapids: Zondervan, 1962), p. 23.
58 Rhodes, p. 66.

It's a fantastic feeling. We came here thinking maybe yes or maybe no and now things are really happening."[59]

A fascinating verse potentially predicting these very things is found in Deuteronomy 33:24. Here, Moses, while saying goodbye to the tribes just prior to his death on Mount Nebo on the plains of Moab, pronounced blessings upon and made predictions concerning Israel's tribes. Note Moses' words to the tribe of Asher:

Of Asher he said,
"More blessed than sons is Asher;
May he be favored by his brothers,
And may he dip his foot in oil."

Now this is probably not talking about actual petroleum; or, on the other hand, maybe it is. Regardless of one's conclusion on this matter, we can safely surmise that this is a prophecy about wealth coming to Israel in the last days. As Constable explains: "Asher (v. 24) would benefit from the respect of his brethren and prosperity. His territory on the Mediterranean coast would require fortifications, but God would protect him. Oil is probably a metaphor for prosperity, as elsewhere (cf. 32:13; Job 29:6)."[60] According to Ezekiel 38:12 this wealth will furnish the motivation for the attack. So both anti-Semitism and the desire for covetous control of what Israel owns capture the motive for the coming invasion. This conclusion represents the best textual answer to the "Why?" question.

59 Globes Correspondent, "*Huge Oil Discovery on Golan Heights*," <http://www.globes.co.il/en/article-huge-oil-discovery-on-golan-heights-1001071698>; Internet; accessed 9 October 2015.
60 Thomas L. Constable, "Notes on Deuteronomy," <www.soniclight.com>; Internet; accessed 27 May, 2015; p. 125.

CHAPTER

5

What?

Now let's move on to the "What?" question. What is going to happen? What is the predicted aftermath of this invasion? What will be its lingering consequences? What will be the aftereffects and outcome of all these things? Ezekiel 38:19–22 answers these very questions:

> "In My zeal and in My blazing wrath I declare *that* on that day there will surely be a great earthquake in the land of Israel. The fish of the sea, the birds of the heavens, the beasts of the field, all the creeping things that creep on the earth, and all the men who are on the face of the earth will shake at My presence; the mountains also will be thrown down, the steep pathways will collapse and every wall will fall to the ground. I will call for a sword against him on all My mountains," declares the Lord GOD. "Every man's sword will be against his brother. With pestilence and with blood I will enter into judgment with him; and I will rain on him and on his troops, and on the many peoples who are with him, a torrential rain, with hailstones, fire and brimstone."

These verses describe several consequences.[61] The Bible is clear that this invading coalition of nations will be supernaturally annihilated by God. In these verses, Ezekiel predicts that there will both an earthquake and also infighting amongst the invaders. In other words, these nations will start to fight each other as God throws them into a state of confusion. In Judges 7, this is exactly how God defeated the Midianites during the days of Gideon. Judges 7:22 says, "The LORD set the sword of one against another even throughout the whole army." Since the Midianites began to slay one another, Gideon had to do little, if any, actual fighting. In addition, disease will break out. There will also be manifest *torrential rain, hailstones, fire* and burning sulfur.

The aftermath will follow. As mentioned earlier, the birds and the beasts will feast upon the carnage (Ezek. 39:4–5, 17–20). It will take seven months to bury the dead (Ezek. 39:11–12, 14–16). There will also be a seven-year burning of weapons (Ezek. 39:9–10). As also mentioned earlier, many argue that this battle must happen before the tribulation starts. They contend that if you put this invasion in the tribulation period itself, once the seven years have started, mathematically speaking you also would have to have weapons burning during the millennium. Thus, they maintain that the battle must happen before the seven-year tribulation begins so that the weapons can all be burned before the millennium starts. This way there will be no weapons burning during the millennium. Regarding the problem associated with weapons burning during the millennium, I ask, Why is that a problem? Why cannot weapons be burned during the millennium? Of the destruction of Babylon (Rev. 14:8; 16:19; 17:1–19:6), Revelation 19:3 records, "Hallelujah! HER SMOKE RISES UP FOREVER AND EVER." Thus, Babylon will be burning throughout the millennial kingdom. If this is so, then why cannot a few weapons also burn for a mere seven years during the millennial age?

Regardless, the final outcome will be Israel's restoration. From that time onward the nation of Israel will know the Lord. They will be regenerated

---

61 Hitchcock, *Middle East Burning: Is the Spreading Unrest a Sign of the Times?*, pp. 86–87.

as promised by God Himself in the New Covenant (Jer. 31:31–34). Ezekiel 39:22 says, "And the house of Israel will know that I am the Lord their God from that day onward." Ezekiel 39:29 indicates that the Spirit will come upon Israel, "'I will not hide My face from them any longer, for I will have poured out My Spirit on the house of Israel,' declares the Lord God." This result explains why Ezekiel includes all that information in the restoration section of his book (Ezek. 33–48). The Gog-Magog invasion will be the tool that God will use to restore His chosen nation back to Himself. Dyer explains:

> Israel has been trampled underfoot by her enemies, but God will intervene in the future to insure her safety. He will defend His people and judge her enemies in distant countries. . . . The defeat of Gog will also hasten God's plans to restore the other Israelites from other nations. Verses 25–29 look ahead to the end of the Tribulation when God will restore the nation from her final dispersion. . . . The ultimate result of the battle with Gog will be Israel's national repentance and spiritual restoration. This will be fulfilled in the millennial kingdom.[62]

Ezekiel 38 and 39 represent the worst war that will ever occur in Israel's history. Yet, through it all, God will prove Himself faithful as He protects His elect nation at her darkest hour. Why will He do so? Israel has something that no other nation in the history of the world has ever had. Israel has a Divine covenant from God (Gen. 15:18). Thus the prophet Jeremiah, in Jeremiah 31:35–37, says:

> Thus says the Lord,
> Who gives the sun for light by day
> And the fixed order of the moon and the stars for light by night,
> Who stirs up the sea so that its waves roar;
> The Lord of hosts is His name:
> "If this fixed order departs
> From before Me," declares the Lord,
> "Then the offspring of Israel also will cease
> From being a nation before Me forever."
> Thus says the Lord,

---

62 Dyer, pp. 1,299 and 1,302.

"If the heavens above can be measured
And the foundations of the earth searched out below,
Then I will also cast off all the offspring of Israel
For all that they have done," declares the LORD.

Consequently, if the enemies of God want to wipe out Israel, they should stop aiming their rockets and bombs at Israel. Rather, they should aim them at the sun, moon and stars. Because God has made a Divine, unconditional, unilateral covenant with Israel, as long as the sun, moon and the stars or the fixed order exists, Israel will always exist before Him.

CHAPTER

6

How?

A t this point, we are attempting to answer the "How?" question. How is the world that we are living in currently being set up for this very attack predicted in Ezekiel 38 and 39? There are *three* strategic trends presently at work in our world that are aggressively setting the stage for this coming invasion.

Israel's Regathering in Unbelief

The *first* trend involves Israel's present regathering in unbelief. How can you have an attack against Israel in unbelief unless there exists first an Israel in unbelief to attack? So obviously you have to have a regathering of Israel in order to properly set the stage for the Gog and Magog invasion. This very regathering has begun and is continuing to happen in our very own lifetimes. Earlier, we articulated the two predicted eschatological regatherings of Israel: one in unbelief in preparation for the tribulation period and the second one in faith in preparation for millennial blessing. The first regathering in unbelief is currently well underway.

Many reject the notion that the modern state of Israel represents a work of God on the grounds that Israel is in unbelief at the present time.[63] They ask, "How can you see the hand of God in the modern state of Israel? Don't you understand that those people over there in that land are a bunch of Christ-rejecters?" In response to this assertion, I have often heard Thomas Ice respond, "Guess what you have to be before you can be a believer? You have to be an unbeliever, right?" Was not God at work in our lives before we believed in Jesus? I know that God was at work in my life before I believed. He was setting up circumstances, conversations, the condition of my heart, etc. The Scriptures reveal that the Spirit is also at work in our lives prior to our regeneration by convicting us of our need to believe in Jesus (John 16:7–11). If we recognize the hand of God in our lives prior to salvation, then why cannot the same kind of thing also be happening for the nation of Israel today despite her present unbelieving state?

This view regarding the significance of the modern state of Israel is nothing new for traditional dispensational interpreters. Note the following quotes by prophecy scholar John F. Walvoord back in 1962 as he reflected upon the prophetic significance of the modern state of Israel. Keep in mind that he made these statements five years before the Six-Day War liberating Jerusalem and many of Israel's current territories.

> Of the many peculiar phenomena which characterize the present genera-
> tion, few events can claim equal significance as far as Biblical prophecy
> is concerned with that of the return of Israel to their land. It constitutes
> a preparation for the end of the age, the setting for the coming of the
> Lord for His church, and the fulfillment of Israel's prophetic destiny.[64]

Walvoord further explains:

---

63 John Piper, "Land Divine?: We Should Treat the Israeli-Palestinian Dispute as We
    Would Any Other," *World*, May 11, 2002. See also John Piper, "Israel, Palestine,
    and the Middle East," <http://www.desiringgod.org/sermons/israel-palestine-and-
    the-middle-east>; Internet; accessed 29 May 2015.
64 Walvoord, *Israel in Prophecy*, p. 26.

The third and final dispersion began in A.D. 70, with the destruction of Jerusalem and the desecration of the entire land which followed in the next century. From this dispersion, Israel has begun to return in the twentieth century as witnessed in the establishment of the nation Israel. Two million of these people are now established in their ancient land. The present regathering being witnessed by our generation is the largest movement of the people of Israel since the days of Moses, and may be understood to be the beginning of that which will be completed subsequent to the second coming of Christ and the establishment of His kingdom on earth.[65]

Elsewhere, Walvoord similarly noted:

The partial restoration of the nation of Israel to their ancient land in the middle of the 20th century should be recognized by all careful students of the Bible as a most remarkable event. It seems to be a token that God is about to fulfill His Word concerning the glorious future of His chosen people. As has been pointed out in previous discussion, the return of Israel to their ancient land and the establishment of the state of Israel is the first step in a sequence of events which will culminate in Christ's millennial kingdom on earth. The present return of Israel is the prelude and will be followed by the dark hour of their suffering in the great tribulation. This will be succeeded by the return of Christ, the establishment of Christ's kingdom on earth, and the exaltation of the people of Israel to a place of prominence and blessing.[66]

As Walvoord reiterates:

One of the most dramatic evidences that the end of the age is approaching is the fact that Israel has re-established her position as a nation in her ancient land. Israel today is in the proper place to enter into the covenant anticipated in Daniel 9:27 which will begin the last seven-year period leading up to the second coming of Christ. Even the modern city of Jerusalem built by Israel is occupying the precise area predicted in Jeremiah 31:38–40 and constitutes a fulfillment of this prophecy given twenty-five hundred years ago and never before fulfilled.... The fact that in our day there is again movement and development in relation to this ancient nation is a sign that the stage is being set for the final world drama. Certainly as Israel's promises are being fulfilled before our eyes other aspects of prophecy such as the resurrection of the dead in Christ

---

65 Ibid., p. 73.
66 Ibid., p. 115.

and the translation of living saints become a real and an imminent possibility. The hope of Israel is also the hope of the church.[67]

Furthermore, the modern state of Israel represents one of the most obvious and greatest miracles of God. How many Amalekites or Jebusites do you know? The Amalekites and Jebusites are mentioned in the Bible right alongside Israel. Why do we not we see any Amalekites or Jebusites today? The answer to this question lies in the fact that when a nation is removed from its homeland, within a few generations it simply assimilates into the host culture. Consequently, it loses its language, culture, religion and identity.[68]

By contrast, Israel was out of its homeland from A.D. 70 until 1948 and the distinct entity known as the Jews never ceased from existing. Israel returned to the same land from which they were dispossessed nearly 2,000 years earlier with their language, culture, ethnicity and religion intact. Something like this peculiar sociological phenomenon pertaining to the Jews has never happened before. People often ask, "Why does God not perform miracles today?" Whenever you see a Jew you are looking at a modern-day miracle of God. All things being equal, such a person should not exist and neither should an entire nation of them. So we clearly see that this present end-time regathering of Israel in unbelief is a key strategic trend that is currently setting the stage for the looming Gog and Magog war.

A Hostile Coalition of Nations

The *second* strategic trend that we are currently seeing is a present gathering of a coalition of nations with a hostile intent towards Israel. Before we comment specifically on how individual nations are fitting into Ezekiel's prophetic blueprint, let us first offer some general observations about the nations that will be involved in the Gog and Magog war.

---

67   Ibid., pp. 130–31. For similar citations by Walvoord regarding the prophetic significance of the modern state of Israel, also see pp. 67, 97 and 113.

68   Josh McDowell and Don Stewart, *Answers to Tough Questions Skeptics Ask About the Christian Faith* (San Bernardino: Here's Life, 1980), pp. 31–33.

The Motive Provided by Islam

Recall the nine countries that Ezekiel names (Ezek. 38:1–7), as we saw when we were previously answering the "Who?" question. We identified those nations by using the scholarly method. With the possible exception of *Rosh*, what do all of them have in common? The answer is that all of them are Islamic. God loves Muslims and they are souls for whom Christ died. There are many Muslims God wants to reach with the gospel. I am not criticizing them. Rather, I am criticizing here the false doctrine and hateful ideology that enslaves them.

It is important to realize that Islam itself furnishes the motivation for the coming Ezekiel 38 and 39 invasion. Why? In Islam, Jerusalem is the city from which Mohammed supposedly ascended back to Allah. In the Quran, the word "Jerusalem" is not even found a single time. On the other hand, in the Bible, the word "Jerusalem" or "Zion" is used around 1,000 times. Yet, despite this conspicuous absence, Islam still sees Jerusalem as a holy site. According to Islamic doctrine, once Islam has ruled over a territory it irrevocably belongs to Allah. Consequently, any nation that exists (besides an Islamic nation) over a territory that Islam has once ruled is viewed as a usurper and disrespecter of Allah. This theological reality explains why Israel does not even appear on most modern-day Islamic maps. In fact, when Ahmadinejad, the former leader of Iran, voiced his ambition to "wipe [Israel] off the map," he was at least acknowledging that Israel had a place on the map to begin with. Most consistent Muslims will not even go that far.

Consequently, Islam itself will never be satisfied until Israel is removed completely as a nation from the land that is now hers. The modern state of Israel is about the size of the state of New Jersey. She controls far less than one percent of all Middle Eastern territory. She is also, as the only democracy in the region, surrounded by numerous hostile Islamic dictatorships. Most of her neighbors are known practitioners of terrorism and they perpetually threaten to drive Israel into the Mediterranean Sea. The website "Middle East Facts" puts things into proper perspective when it says:

Unlike Islam's Koran, which commands Muslims to force the entire planet to submit to literal control by Islam, the Jewish Torah promises the children of Israel a modest and reasonable allotment of land. Israel . . . is a democratic nation 1/19th the size of California, surrounded by 22 hostile Arab/Islamic dictatorships with 640 times her size, 60 times her population and ALL the oil. How dare Arab propagandists call Israel "expansionist!" And how dare anyone believe them! How can Israel, which occupies one-sixth of one percent of the lands called Arab, be responsible for the political dissatisfaction of 22 Arab countries? How can the 13 million Jews in the world (almost 5 million fewer than they were in 1939!) be blamed for the problems of the 250 million Arabs, who have brotherly ties to 1.4 billion Muslims worldwide? Israel is an oasis of Western Democracy and Judeo/Christian morality in the middle of an otherwise totalitarian Arab/Muslim Middle East. For over 55 years since she became a nation in 1948, Israel has sought peaceful coexistence with neighbors dedicated to her destruction. Thus far only Egypt and Jordan have formalized a peace treaty. In reality, these two peace treaties are questionable.[69]

Yet, what are the world community and the Islamic world constantly communicating? Israel needs to give up just a little bit more territory consecutively for peace to finally exist in the region. This is known as the "land for peace" process. Does a "land for peace" policy with hostile neighbors bent on your destruction actually lead to lasting peace? All one needs to do to refute the notion that appeasement is effective at bringing peace is to recall that Israel withdrew from the Gaza Strip in 2005. Those in Gaza then elected Hamas to power in 2007 and used this territory as a beachhead to launch countless rockets into Israeli territory during the summer of 2014. Giveaways of a small portion of Israeli land in exchange for the illusory promise of peace will never satisfy Islam. Rather, such appeasement will only be perceived as weakness and embolden Islam's aggression since Islam is actually interested in seizing all of Israel's land rather than just a small portion of it.

Lest the reader think this to be an overgeneralization, recall Camp David 2000 during the waning days of the Clinton administration when Palestine Liberation Organization Chairman Yasser Arafat was offered

69   <http://www.mefacts.com/cached.asp?x_id=10190>; Internet; accessed 27 May 2015.

on a silver platter most of Israel's "disputed" territories. Mitchell Bard well explains the deal that was offered to and rejected by the Arabs:

> In 2000, Israeli Prime Minister Ehud Barak offered to withdraw from 97 percent of the West Bank and 100 percent of the Gaza Strip. In addition, he agreed to dismantle 63 isolated settlements. In exchange for the 3 percent annexation of the West Bank, Israel said it would give up territory in the Negev that would increase the size of the Gaza territory by roughly a third. Barak also made previously unthinkable concessions on Jerusalem, agreeing that Arab neighborhoods of East Jerusalem would become the capital of the new state. The Palestinians would maintain control over their holy places and have "religious sovereignty" over the Temple Mount. According to U.S. peace negotiator Dennis Ross, Israel offered to create a Palestinian state that was contiguous, and not a series of cantons. Even in the case of the Gaza Strip, which must be physically separate from the West Bank unless Israel were to be cut into non-contiguous pieces, a solution was devised whereby an overland highway would connect the two parts of the Palestinian state without any Israeli checkpoints or interference. The proposal also addressed the Palestinian refugee issue, guaranteeing them the right of return to the Palestinian state and reparations from a $30 billion fund that would be collected from international donors to compensate them. Arafat was asked to agree to Israeli sovereignty over the parts of the Western Wall religiously significant to Jews (i.e., not the entire Temple Mount), and three early warning stations in the Jordan Valley, which Israel would withdraw from after six years. Most important, however, Arafat was expected to agree that the conflict with Israel was over at the end of the negotiations. This was the true deal breaker. Arafat was not willing to end the conflict . . . . The prevailing view of the Camp David/White House negotiations—that Israel offered generous concessions, and that Yasser Arafat rejected them to pursue the war that began in September 2000—was acknowledged for more than a year. To counter the perception that Arafat was the obstacle to peace, the Palestinians and their supporters then began to suggest a variety of excuses for why Arafat failed to say "yes" to a proposal that would have established a Palestinian state. The truth is that if the Palestinians were dissatisfied with any part of the Israeli proposal, all they had to do was offer a counterproposal. They never did.[70]

If your sincere motive is truly "land for peace," then why turn down such an unprecedented deal? The simple answer is that Islam is not interested in a part of Israel, but rather the entire land. Islam will

---

70 Mitchell Bard, "Myths and Facts: A Guide to the Arab-Israeli Conflict," <http://www.jewishvirtuallibrary.org/jsource/myths3/MFpeace.html>; Internet; accessed 27 May 2015.

never rest as long as Israel exists in any form or substance. Benjamin Netanyahu captures this sentiment, when he says: "If the Arabs put down their weapons today, there would be no more violence. If the Jews put down their weapons today, there would be no more Israel."

Interestingly, the PLO was founded in 1964. Why is this date so significant? The Palestine Liberation Organization is now known as the Palestinian Authority, and today attempts to convey that its only goal is merely to roll back Israel's land to its pre-1967 borders. In 1967, during the Six-Day War, Israel's borders increased. Thus, the PLO gives the impression that if Israel will simply go back to its pre-1967 borders, then they will be content. If this is so, then why was the organization founded in 1964, three years before Israel received her expanded borders? What exactly was the PLO trying to liberate in 1964? In other words, noting the PLO's founding date leads to the obvious conclusion that the organization's ultimate goal is not merely to decrease Israel's land to its pre-1967 borders, but rather to eradicate the state of Israel itself.

The very nations that Ezekiel foresaw, we see constantly in today's headlines. Many of them were participants in the so-called "Arab Spring," which began in 2010. Essentially, the Arab Spring was all about replacing one moderate Middle Eastern Arabic government after another with a more radical form of an Islamic dictatorship. Our former president, George W. Bush, called this very coalition of nations the "axis of evil." There is a dominant idea in Islam called *caliphate*, which refers to worldwide submission to Islamic *Sharia* Law. This word *caliphate* is found in the *Quran Surah* (or chapter) 24:55. This passage says:

> Allah has promised those who have believed among you and done righteous deeds that He will surely grant them succession [Caliphate] upon the earth just as He granted it to those before them and that He will surely establish for them [therein] their religion which He has preferred for them and that He will surely substitute for them, after their fear, security, [for] they worship Me, not associating anything with Me. But whoever disbelieves after that - then those are the defiantly disobedient.

In essence, this passage is a revelation of Islam's true ambition for worldwide control. All of these things indicate that the very nations are in place that Ezekiel foresaw some 2,600 years ago. We are witnessing the gathering of a coalition of Middle Eastern nations with a hostile intent toward Israel. Islam exerts great influence over these nations. Thus, Islam, both in its desire to eradicate Israel as well its lust for worldwide domination, furnishes the motive for this coming attack.

Persia or Iran

Let us focus now more specifically on just a few of the nations in the invading coalition that Ezekiel mentions in order to demonstrate how Ezekiel's prophecy is shaping up in our day. Recall that we indicated that *Persia* represents modern-day Iran. When Ezekiel initially received his prophecy back in the sixth century B.C., *Persia* was actually a friend rather than a foe of Israel. After all, it was *Persia* under Cyrus and later Artaxerxes that allowed the Jews to return home after the 70-year captivity in three successive waves as recorded in the post-exilic books of Ezra and Nehemiah. So Ezekiel's prophecies regarding *Persia* turning against Israel probably seemed improbable—if not impossible—at least to Ezekiel himself. They also probably seemed unlikely to most westerners prior to 1979 since at that time *Persia*, or Iran, was an ally of both America and Israel. However, everything shifted with the deposing of the Shah in 1979. At that point, when the Shah was deposed and replaced by the Ayatollah and Iran was Islamicized during the days of Jimmy Carter, who is broadly considered one of America's weakest Presidents, Iran took on a totally different posture. While the Shah was a well-known human rights violator, at least under his watch Iran was a somewhat progressive and modern country. Today, Iran is a repressive Shiite Muslim dictatorship and regime and is perhaps the world's most aggressive sponsor of worldwide terrorism. In sum, although Ezekiel's prophecies seemed absurd in Ezekiel's day and even prior to 1979, yet in our day Ezekiel's prophetic scenario has begun to appear credible.

It is breathtaking to observe the speed at which Iran is moving into the very prophetic alignment spoken of by the exilic prophet Ezekiel. Ahmadinejad, the former leader of Iran, is both a Holocaust denier and a *twelver*. As a Shiite Muslim, he argues that the twelfth Imam will return to earth during a time of great warfare, which he believes he can hasten through the destruction of the great Satan, the United States of America, and the little Satan, Israel. Notice the order: the United States of America is the great Satan, and Israel is the little Satan. Recall that it was Ahmadinejad who, at his "World Without Zionism" Conference in Tehran in 2005, voiced his ambition to "wipe [Israel] off the map." Ahmadinejad was replaced in August of 2013 by Rouhani, who is currently being promoted to the world community as a moderate. Rouhani's moderate image makes him even more dangerous than Ahmadinejad. Rouhani is far less overt and clandestine in his true intentions toward Israel and the rest of the world. Such a leadership approach makes it more difficult for the world community to identify as dangerous. Under Rouhani, Iran's nuclear program has accelerated and not slowed down. Even as I write, Iran inches ever closer to the nuclear finish line.

In fact, one of the greatest facilitators that accelerated the prospect of Iran's crossing the nuclear finish line was the Obama Administration. Toward the end of his second term, Obama seemed hell-bent on pursuing his ambition of securing his own legacy in the annals of history by entering into a historic and unprecedented deal with Iran. This agreement called for lifting ". . . Western sanctions on Iran in exchange for the country dropping from 19,000 to 5,060 active centrifuges, limiting its highly enriched uranium, and increasing inspections."[71] However, Israeli Prime Minister Benjamin Netanyahu correctly pointed out, this agreement was a "bad deal." He explained:

> It does not roll back Iran's nuclear program. It keeps a vast nuclear infrastructure in place. Not a single centrifuge is destroyed. Not a single nuclear facility is shut down, including the underground

---

71   Eric Bradner, "Netanyahu: More Iran Options Than 'This Bad Deal or War,'" <http://www.cnn.com/2015/04/05/politics/netanyahu-iran-deal/>; Internet; accessed 27 May 2015.

facilities that they built illicitly. Thousands of centrifuges will keep spinning, enriching uranium. That's a very bad deal. . . . I think that we can have a legitimate difference of opinion on this, because I think Iran has shown to be completely distrustful . . . [and a nation guilty of] congenital cheating.[72]

Can Iran be trusted with a nuclear weapon? To properly answer this question, one need look no further than the Iranian children's indoctrination through their public school textbooks. Retired ambassador and consultant Yoram Ettinger offers the following helpful and frightening insight:

> Iranian school textbooks, such as The Qur'an and Life (Grade 12, p. 125) prepare Iranian children for the Ayatollahs' sublime goal: the apocalyptic, horrifying, millenarian, military battle against the USA and other "arrogant oppressors of the world," which are ostensibly led by "idolatrous devils." While the "savior" — the infallible, immortal, divinely ordained and eventual global leader, the Mahdi — has not surfaced yet, Iranian children are taught that the battle is already raging throughout the world, awaiting their sacrifice. School textbooks of Western democracies are the most authentic reflection of peoples' values and worldview. School textbooks of tyrannies are the most authentic reflection of the nature and mission of the regimes. Iranian school textbooks reflect the strategy and tactics of the Ayatollahs, much more authentically than speeches, interviews, diplomatic statements and conversations conducted by President Rouhani and Foreign Minister Zarif. The latter have mastered the art of Quran-sanctioned Taqiyya — doubletalk and deception-based agreements, aimed at shielding the "believers" from the "disbelievers," to be abrogated once conditions are ripe. School textbooks are considered, by the Ayatollahs, a critical means to mobilize the youth, charting the roadmap to the final military victory over the infidel USA and the West. Hence, the crucial relevance of school textbooks to the Congressional debate on "the framework agreement with Iran" and on the clear and present threat of a nuclear threshold Iran to vital US interests. Therefore, it behooves the US Senate and House of Representatives — the coequal and codetermining branch of government in the area of national security policy — to conduct a series of hearings and colloquy on the significance of Iran's school textbooks, on the nature of Iran's conventional and nuclear threats to US interests, and on the role played by the non-war US military threat/stick, as

---

72 Ibid.

an effective option to prevent a nuclear war. Holding these hearings and colloquy — before an agreement is reached in Lausanne - would constitute a vitamin — not a poison pill — to a constructive agreement, sparing the world a calamitous nuclear war. Prof. Eldad Pardo, of the Hebrew University, who has researched Iran's school textbooks of the last 10 years, published a May, 2015 report for the Institute of Monitoring Peace and Tolerance in School Education. According to Prof. Pardo, "Iran had created a war curriculum to prepare an entire generation for global war, based on Ayatollah Ruhollah Khomeini's vision of collective martyrdom.... The battle between the new Islamic (Iranian) civilization and the evil Western civilization is seen as one between good and evil, and is being waged on a global scale....The school textbooks prepare the Iranian people for a constant state of emergency, requiring Iranians to foment revolutions throughout the world...." Pardo documents the apocalyptic theme in Iran's school textbooks, as underlined by *Defense Readiness* (Grade 11, p. 11), praising more than 500,000 school children, who were sent to the front, during the 1980-88 war against Iraq. According to Robin Wright (*Sacred Rage: The Wrath of Militant Islam*, New York: Simon & Schuster, 2001, p. 37), "they led the way, running over minefields to clear the ground for the Iranian ground assault. Wearing white headbands to signify the embracing of death and shouting: "Shaheed, Shaheed" [Martyr, martyr], they literally blew their way into heaven...." Apocalyptic regimes are induced — not deterred — by Mutual Assured Destruction. Iranian children are prodded to martyrdom, in defiance of their parents: "The defense of Islam and Muslims is a duty, and does not require parents' approval (*Religious Rulings*, Grade 11, p.14)...." Prof. Pardo established that "education to child martyrdom continues during first-twelve grades, with a new emphasis on girl martyrs (*Defense Readiness*, Grade 11, pp. 35 and 62 and *Sociology 1*, Grade 11, pp. 112, 114)." The apocalyptic, millenarian vision of the Ayatollahs is reinforced by Jihad-driven school textbooks: "alongside the fighting jihad, there is a spiritual 'greater jihad' (Jehad-e akbar) performed by the fighter-martyrs (*Defense Readiness*, Grade 11, pp. 28-32)." *Religious Rulings* (Grade 11, p. 12) teaches that the eternal Jihad means a battle in accordance with God's way, in the defense of Muslims and the oppressed. The chapter on "*Defense and Jihad*" stipulates that a battle could mean killing, massacring, murdering and/or fighting. Children are urged to join a millenarian frenzy of military training and preparations, constant emergency, blind obedience and actual participation in conflicts, at home and abroad." Iranian children study that in times of need, dissimulation and deceptive peace pacts — even with 'un-Godly, idolatrous governments' —are proper, but only until such time as the balance of power should change. In fact, we know from Khamenei's own words, that the nuclear negotiations are predicated on the conclusion of a provisional treaty with an illegitimate [infidel] government, while not forsaking the permanent vision. Khamenei's conduct is based on the 661 CE Treaty between Imam Hassan and Caliph Mu'awiyah, intending only to gain time, building power and gradually undermining rival dynasties— but never genuinely reconciling (*Religion and Life, Grade 12*, p. 104)." Thus, school textbooks constitute a very accurate detector of the nature, mission and legitimacy/illegitimacy of regimes, and their expected use of nuclear capabilities.[73]

In addition to examining the textbooks that Iranian school children are routinely propagandized with, the pernicious motives of the Iranian government is also nakedly revealed by the books authored by its own leadership. A recently-published 416-page book authored by Iran's leader, the Ayatollah Ali Khamenei, all but telegraphs Iran's true hostile intentions to the world in general and Israel in particular. Notice Amir Taheri's analysis of this book that was recently sent to him by a friend:

While Secretary of State John Kerry and President Obama do their best to paper over the brutality of the Iranian regime and force through a nuclear agreement, Iran's religious leader has another issue on his mind: The destruction of Israel. Ayatollah Ali Khamenei has published a new book called "Palestine," a 416-page screed against the Jewish state. A blurb on the back cover credits Khamenei as "The flag bearer of Jihad to liberate Jerusalem." . . . He uses three words. One is "nabudi," which means "annihilation." The other is "imha," which means "fading out," and, finally, there is "zaval," meaning "effacement." Khamenei claims that his strategy for the destruction of Israel is not based on anti-Semitism, which he describes as a European phenomenon. His position is instead based on "well-established Islamic principles." One such principle is that a land that falls under Muslim rule, even briefly, can never again be ceded to non-Muslims. What matters in Islam is ownership of a land's government, even if the majority of inhabitants are non-Muslims. . . . Dozens of maps circulate in the Muslim world showing the extent of Muslim territories lost to the Infidel that must be recovered. These include large parts of Russia and Europe,

73 Yoram Ettinger, "Iran's School Textbooks—Can Congress Afford to Ignore It?" <http://theettingerreport.com/Iran-and-MidEast/Iran-s-School-Textbooks-%E2%80%93-can-Congress-afford-to-i.aspx, May 29, 2015>; Internet; accessed 30 May 2015.

almost a third of China, the whole of India and parts of the Philippines and Thailand. However, according to Khamenei, Israel, which he labels as "adou" and "doshman," meaning "enemy" and "foe," is a special case for three reasons. The first is that it is a loyal "ally of the American Great Satan" and a key element in its "evil scheme" to dominate "the heartland of the Ummah." The second reason is that Israel has waged war on Muslims on a number of occasions, thus becoming "a hostile infidel," or "kaffir al-harbi." Finally, Israel is a special case because it occupies Jerusalem, which Khamenei describes as "Islam's third Holy City." He intimates that one of his "most cherished wishes" is to one day pray in Jerusalem. Khamenei insists that he is not recommending "classical wars" to wipe Israel off the map. Nor does he want to "massacre the Jews." What he recommends is a long period of low-intensity warfare designed to make life unpleasant if not impossible for a majority of Israeli Jews so that they leave the country. His calculation is based on the assumption that large numbers of Israelis have double nationality and would prefer emigration to the United States and Europe to daily threats of death. Khamenei makes no reference to Iran's nuclear program. But the subtext is that a nuclear-armed Iran would make Israel think twice before trying to counter Khamenei's strategy by taking military action against the Islamic Republic. In Khamenei's analysis, once the cost of staying in Israel has become too high for many Jews, Western powers, notably the US, which have supported the Jewish state for decades, might decide that the cost of doing so is higher than possible benefits. Thanks to President Obama, the US has already distanced itself from Israel to a degree unimaginable a decade ago. Khamenei counts on what he sees as "Israel fatigue." The international community would start looking for what he calls "a practical and logical mechanism" to end the old conflict. Khamenei's "practical and logical mechanism" excludes the two-state formula in any form. "The solution is a one-state formula," he declares. That state, to be called Palestine, would be under Muslim rule but would allow non-Muslims, including some Israeli Jews who could prove "genuine roots" in the region, to stay as "protected minorities." . . . Khamenei describes Israel as "a cancerous tumor" whose elimination would mean that "the West's hegemony and threats will be discredited" in the Middle East. In its place, he boasts, "the hegemony of Iran will be promoted." Khamenei's book also deals with the Holocaust, which he regards either as "a propaganda ploy" or a disputed claim. "If there was such a thing," he writes, "we don't know why it happened and how."[74]

74 Amir Taheri, "Iran Publishes Book on How to Outwit US and Destroy Israel," <http://nypost.com/2015/08/01/iran-publishes-book-on-how-to-outwit-us-and-destroy-israel/, August 1, 2015>; Internet; accessed 18 January 2016.

So here, in written form, we clearly see Iran's naked and true intentions.

FIRST — First, Iran sees Israel as a "cancerous tumor" that must be excised.

SECOND — Second, Israel is an illegitimate state since it resides on real estate once controlled by Islam.

THIRD — Third, the city of Jerusalem actually belongs to Allah rather than to the physical descendants of Abraham, Isaac and Jacob since Jerusalem represents Islam's third holiest city. This claim lacks credibility on its face since the word "Jerusalem" is not found a single time in either the Quran or the Hadith despite the fact that the word is found roughly 800 times in the Hebrew Bible (or what Protestants sometimes flippantly refer to as the Old Testament).

FOURTH — Fourth, the Jewish state is to be viewed with hostility since she is an ally of the Great Satan, the United States of America.

FIFTH — Fifth, an Iranian nuclear program is necessary in order for Iran to intensify its already existing long-term proxy warfare against Israel so as to persuade as many Jews as possible to leave Israel and to dissuade other Jews from immigrating there.

SIXTH — Sixth, any world sympathy for Israel on account of her past persecutions is inappropriate because the Holocaust never really happened in the first place.

All of this encapsulates the true and discernible face of the Iranian regime, if only our leaders would take seriously the recent writings of Kahmenei.

Are these mere writings of dictators an accurate reflection of their true intentions? A study of recent history helps answer this question. In his two-volume book entitled *Mein Kampf* ("My Struggle"), published in 1925–1926, before his ascent to political power, Adolf Hitler meticulously laid out his political ideology and future plans. How different things could have been had the world at that time simply paid attention to Hitler's writings.

In sum, as evidenced by its relatively recent Shiite Muslim trajectory, its nuclear ambitions, what it teaches to its own school children and the written expressions of its own leadership, it is apparent that Iran is fitting into the identical aggressive pattern that Ezekiel predicted regarding *Persia's* end-time role.

Cush or Sudan

Recall that we identified *Cush* as the modern Sudan. *Cush* is the area that actually harbored Osama Bin Laden between 1991 and 1996. As noted by Hitchcock, "Sudan is a hard-line Islamic nation that supported Iraq in the Gulf War and harbored Osama bin Laden from 1991 to 1996."[75] *Cush*, or the modern-day Sudan, is also the place of one of the worst genocides on the globe called the Darfur genocide. As noted by Renald Showers, "Sudan is dominated by a brutal Arab Islamic fundamentalist government that murders, rapes, and enslaves Christians and animists and is slaughtering the black Muslims in Darfur in an attempt to establish a pure Islamic state."[76]

Put or Libya

Earlier we noted that *Put* is modern-day Libya. Libya was the home of the lengthy rule of Muammar Gaddafi, a well-known sponsor of terror:

> On April 5, 1986 three people were killed and around 230 injured when La Belle discothèque was bombed in West Berlin. The entertainment venue was commonly frequented by United States soldiers, and two of the dead and 79 of the injured were American servicemen....

---

75 Hitchcock, "The Battle of Gog and Magog," p. 8.

76 Renald Showers, *The Coming Apocalypse: A Study of Replacement Theology Vs. God's Faithfulness in the End Times* (Bellmawr, NJ: Friends of Israel, 2009), p. 92.

Libya was accused of sponsoring the bombing by the US government, and US President Ronald Reagan ordered retaliatory strikes on Tripoli and Benghazi in Libya ten days later. The strikes reportedly killed at least 15 people, including Colonel Gaddafi's adopted daughter. A 2001 trial in the US found that the bombing had been 'planned by the Libyan secret service and the Libyan Embassy.'[77]

Because of the consistent application of then-United States President Ronald Reagan's "peace through strength" doctrine against sponsors of terrorism, Gaddafi remained largely silent and non-assertive in the subsequent decades. However, as a consequence of the Arab Spring, due to a Muslim Brotherhood-dominated uprising, Gaddafi was deposed as ruler of Libya in 2011 and later assassinated.

Libya began to show up on the radar screens of most Americans on September 11, 2012. Benghazi, Libya is where, on the anniversary of the toppling of the Twin Towers, our embassy was attacked, our ambassador was killed and four Americans lost their lives. An attack of this nature on an American embassy has not transpired since the hostage crisis in Iran in 1979. The Obama administration, in order to deflect criticism for failing to adequately prepare for the obvious and growing threat of danger against our embassy in Benghazi, just a few weeks before a national election, went in front of the American public and repeatedly lied. They blamed the Benghazi incident on a spontaneous uprising caused by an amateur video critical of Islam rather than their own unwillingness to appropriately respond to intelligence reports pointing to growing danger in the area. However, such an explanation strains credulity to the breaking point. Why did the attack at Benghazi happen on 9-11? Why were sophisticated armor and warfare used in this attack? Consequently, how can such an uprising be considered spontaneous and unplanned by Islamic Jihadists?

---

77 <http://en.wikipedia.org/wiki/1986_Berlin_discotheque_bombing>; Internet; accessed 27 May 2015.

Meshech, Tubal, Gomer, Togarmah or Turkey

Recall that we also identified *Meshech, Tubal, Gomer* and *Togarmah* as modern-day Turkey. Turkey was a long-time ally of America and member of NATO. Now, however, Turkey is going the way of Iran. Its secular government is being replaced by an Islamic Republic. Hitchcock observes:

> The climate in Turkey began to shift in 2002 when the AKP (Turkish Justice and Development Party) was swept to power in a landslide victory. This party has exercised increasing influence in the country, turning Turkey from a secular nation to an Islamist one. Turkey has been a secular democratic state since the fall of the Ottoman Empire and the establishment of the Republic of Turkey in 1923. . . . [78]

According to Frank Gaffney, president of the Center for Security Policy, Turkey is transitioning from "a secular democracy with a Muslim society into a state governed by a radical Islamic ideology hostile to Western values and freedoms."[79]

As reported by *Newsweek*, Turkey's transition from Western alliances to Eastern ones was expedited significantly through the ascendency of Turkish Prime Minster Erdogan, who served in that role from 2003 to 2014:

> The fear is that the prime minister could turn away from Turkey's traditional Western alliances and join forces instead with anti-U.S. hardliners in the Middle East. Recently, the nervousness has become more palpable than ever. First, Erdogan teamed up with President Luiz Inácio Lula da Silva of Brazil in an effort to block U.N. sanctions against Iran's nuclear program. And then Erdogan accused Israel of "state-sponsored terrorism" and broke off military ties after an Israeli commando raid on a Turkish flotilla that was carrying aid to Gaza. Turkey has long been America's closest Muslim ally, and its formula for separating mosque and state in a thriving democracy seemed a model for the rest of the region. . . . What worries Turkey's Western allies most, though, is Erdogan's chumminess with the likes of Mahmoud Ahmadinejad. Scenes of Erdogan embracing the Iranian president this May and calling him "my good friend" drove the White House wild. . . . On a gut level,

---

78 Hitchcock, *Middle East Burning: Is the Spreading Unrest a Sign of the Times?*, pp. 139–40.

79 Frank Gaffney, *War Footing* (Annapolis: Naval Institute Press, 2006), p. 164; as cited in Rhodes, 177.

Erdogan feels "more comfortable in Tehran or Moscow than Brussels or Washington," says Ian Lesser of the German Marshall Fund of the United States. . . . That stance, combined with Erdogan's fiery remarks about Turkey's former ally Israel—calling Gaza a "prison camp" and denying that Hamas is a terrorist organization—have made him a hero to many Arabs.[80]

At the time of the following statement, Erdogan served as Turkey's president while Davutoglu served as the country's prime minister. Yet, during that era, the rhetoric from these leaders never abated. If anything, it intensified significantly and, in fact, sounded eerily similar to Ezekiel's prophetic description.

The amazing speeches by Turkish President Recep Tayyip Erdogan and Prime Minister Ahmet Davutoglu were given at the inauguration ceremony at the country's 55th airport in Yuksekova district of southeastern border province of Hakkari, in which they made an entire declaration to the Islamic world, on their desire to conquer Jerusalem and form a universal Islamic empire. . . . In the conference Davutoglu declared the universally Islamic aspiration to conquer Jerusalem: 'By Allah's will, Jerusalem belongs to the Kurds, the Turks, the Arabs, and to all Muslims. And as our forefathers fought side by side at Gallipoli, and just as our forefathers went together to liberate Jerusalem with Saladin, we will march together on the same path [to liberate Jerusalem].' Again, here we have the prime minister, with Erdogan, declaring the Islamic desire to conquer Jerusalem. This desire to retake Jerusalem is the same sentiment that the Muslims of the Middle Ages were fighting to fulfill. Now that Turkey wants to pursue this very same conquests, it is obvious that we are going back to Medieval Times. They are praising Saladin who fought a very fierce battle with Richard the Lionheart in the *Battle of Acre*, in which the Christians won, and who defeated the Christians in the *Battle of Jerusalem*, and they are also speaking of the Battle of Gallipoli, in which the Muslims defeated the Christian English.[81]

---

80 Owen Matthews, "Should Turkey's Erdogan Worry the West?" <http://www. newsweek.com/should-turkeys-erdogan-worry-west-72021, September 11, 2010>; Internet; accessed 29 May 2015.

81 "Turkish President and PM: 'We Will Gather Together All Of The Muslim World and Invade Jerusalem,'" <htmlhttp://www.israelislamandendtimes.com/ turkish-president-and-pm-we-will-gather-together-all-of-the-muslim-world-and-invade-jerusalem/, May 30, 2015>; Internet; accessed 30 May 2015.

Interestingly, both Davutoglu and Erdogan denied that Jerusalem was once a Jewish city beginning with the David's conquest of this ancient city from the Jebusites back in 1000 B.C. (2 Sam. 5). Burak Bekdil observes:

> It is truly fascinating that Turkey's Prime Minister Ahmet Davutoglu, a professor of political science, believes that Jerusalem, built a millennium before the birth of Islam, is originally a Muslim city.... It is as if, for Davutoglu (and Erdogan), Jerusalem did not exist before 1187.... President Erdogan has no less-eccentric ideas. "Jerusalem," according to the president, "is the holiest place of Muslims and it belongs to the Palestinians."[82]

Certainly such historical revisionism would increase Turkey's ambition to contribute to the coming invasion since it converts the Jews presently living in the ancient city into usurpers.

Turkish leadership at times even seems transparent in harboring the very anti-Semitic motivation that will serve as the catalyst for the upcoming Gog–Magog invasion. Recently, Erdogan went so far as to express his admiration for Adolf Hitler's Nazi Germany. Political science professor John A. Tures, writing for the *Huffington Post*, reports:

> Late Friday afternoon, reports circulated that Erdogan expressed admiration for Adolf Hitler's Nazi government. If it was a statement made by a democratic figure, it would be treated as a gaffe or bad joke in poor taste. But for the authoritarian Erdogan, it's a rare instance of his honesty, showing how the strongman really feels. *Business Insider* reported on the links Erdogan made between his vision of the new Turkish government that he is pushing for, and Hitler's regime. "Asked on his return from a visit to Saudi Arabia late on Thursday whether an executive presidential system was possible while maintaining the unitary structure of the state, he said: 'There are already examples in the world. You can see it when you look at Hitler's Germany. There are later examples in various other countries,' he told reporters, according to a recording broadcast by the Dogan news agency." ... Of course, in Erdogan's Hitleresque state, it would be a crime to suggest that Erdogan admired Hitler. Ironically, you could even be marched off to prison, for suggesting that Erdogan is

---

82   Burak Bekdil, "Turkish Fairy Tales from Uncle Tayyip," <http://www.gatestoneinstitute.org/5843/erdogan-fairy-tales, May 20, 2015>; Internet; accessed 31 May 2015.

authoritarian. In fact, Erdogan's government has arrested many people, including journalists and law enforcement officials of uncovering evidence of corruption or accusing him of authoritarian actions. He even targeted people living in the USA who are critical of him. Erdogan's excuse for such actions is that he claims his enemies are "terrorists." Turkey's social media, one of the few unregulated sources of news in Erdogan's government, immediately went into high gear, according to the *New York Times*: "Let's do a close comparison between Hitler and Erdogan," one person wrote on Twitter. "The only difference is that Hitler was a bit shorter." People also shared a Photoshopped picture of Hitler with Mr. Erdogan's face superimposed on it. On a visit to Turkey during their June election, I found that the overwhelming majority of people I met really like their democratic system. Many didn't like Erdogan, but were afraid to say anything. Of those who did, half asked me to keep it anonymous, while the other half said they would be arrested anyway, and it didn't matter if I used their names. Despite his party's win in the November election, Erdogan's ruling AKP does not have the votes to give their leader the Hitleresque power that he wants. But he is seeking a referendum to get those powers, which would likely ensure that Erdogan and his family will rule this NATO ally of the USA indefinitely, in a most undemocratic manner. Should the United States break diplomatic relations with Erdogan's regime, help Turkey's civil society, review possible cuts to U.S. military aid to Turkey's government, or consider "smart sanctions" against Erdogan and his family? Erdogan's admission of admiration for Hitler demonstrates that doing nothing will not help the problem, any more than it did in the 1930s.[83]

As Turkey shifts alliances away from the West, she is forming greater alliances with the identical nations anticipated in Ezekiel's prophesied coalition. Maughan notes:

> In late May of 2010 the top leaders from Russia, Iran, and Turkey met together at a summit in Turkey to discuss strengthening the ties and alliances between them as nations. So right before our eyes, Turkey seems to be shifting its alliance from the West to the very nations Ezekiel lists in this confederacy. Turkey now endorses Iran's nuclear program and international defiance, and is joining in denouncing Israel.[84]

83 John A. Tures, "It's No Surprise That Turkey's Erdogan Likes Adolf Hitler's Government," <http://www.huffingtonpost.com/john-a-tures/its-no-surprise-that-turk_b_8903734.html, January 4, 2016>; Internet; accessed 18 January 2016.
84 Maughan, p. 50.

At the time of writing, Turkey has again sought admission into the European Union.[85] However, in recent history, Turkey's hopes have been dashed for admission to the European Union. This general pattern of denial seems to indicate that Turkey will continue to become anti-western, Islamicize and cooperate with this hostile coalition of nations spoken of in Ezekiel 38 and 39. Hitchcock explains, "In recent years Turkey has made every attempt to become part of the European Union. For this reason Turkey's participation in the Gog alliance against Israel appeared highly unlikely. However, it now appears certain that the EU will reject Turkey's bid for admission."[86]

Turkey's one-time status as an ally of Israel has also been significantly altered in recent days. Evidence of Turkeys' hostile relationship with Israel is illustrated by the flotilla that was dispatched from Turkey to break Israel's blockade of Gaza on May 31, 2010. Thus, Maughan observes:

> All this was before the infamous confrontation with a Turkish ship attempting to break Israel's blockade of Gaza on May 31, 2010. Contrary to how this was portrayed in the mainstream media, this event had nothing to do with humanitarian aid, but everything to do with the politics of the region. Through this event, Turkey turned on Israel quite viciously, and relations between the two countries have almost completely fallen apart. This could be one more indication that the war of Gog and Magog is drawing close. It demonstrates a major change of direction for the country of Turkey.[87]

In sum, while the Turkish alignment with Ezekiel's Islamic anti-Israel coalition seemed virtually impossible just a few years ago, now even Turkey is fitting exactly into prophetic alignment.

---

85 Danny Kemp, "Turkey Relaunches EU bid as Part of Migrant Deal," <http://news.yahoo.com/turkey-eu-open-chapter-membership-talks-officials-173449046.html, December 15, 2015>; Internet; accessed 18 January 2016.
86 Hitchcock, "The Battle of Gog and Magog," p. 28.
87 Maughan, p. 49.

Rosh or Russia

Earlier we identified *Rosh* as Russia. For many years Ezekiel's prophecies about *Rosh's* invasion seemed absurd. Russia seemed harmless given the fact that it was considered a Christian Orthodox country. According to *Wikipedia*, "The state adopted Christianity from the Byzantine Empire in 988, beginning the synthesis of Byzantine and Slavic cultures that defined Russian culture for the next millennium."[88] Yet, the character of the nation eventually changed beginning with the Communist Revolution in Russia in 1917 and the eventual rise of the Soviet Union as a nuclear superpower. We well remember Russia from the Cold War days and its expansionistic policies. Then, after the Soviet Union collapsed, we were promised that a new era of peace had arrived as *Glasnost* and *Perestroika* were being aggressively promoted by Russian leader Mikhail Gorbachev and the rest of the world community. Yet, in 2008 the Russian bear suddenly awoke from its slumber, got hungry again, and consequently rolled right over the neighboring country of Georgia. More recently, in 2014, we have witnessed Russian aggressiveness and expansionism in the Ukrainian territory of Crimea. How interesting that Ezekiel foresaw the aggressive character and nature of *Rosh* 2,600 years ago.

Russia is arguably the one country in Ezekiel's predicted last-days coalition that currently seems the least influenced by Islam. Yet, given the vast Muslim population growth in Russia, there is a credible argument to be made that even Russia itself is becoming increasingly Islamicized. Showers explains:

> Present trends indicate that, unless things change in the near future, Russia will become an Islamic majority state within several decades. Russian people are not propagating enough children to maintain the Russian population in their native country. Many younger Russian women refused to have children. The majority of those who do, limit themselves to one child. A high Russian abortion rate contributes to this trend. Demographers who study population growth predict that, if this trend continues, the Russian population will decline from 143 million to 100 million by 2050. By contrast, almost all Muslim couples in Russia

---

88 <http://en.wikipedia.org/wiki/History_of_Russia>; Internet; accessed 27 May 2015.

have three to five children. Consequently, in Russia the Muslim population growth since 1989 is between 40 and 50 percent. In 1991 there were 300 mosques in Russia. In 2006 there were approximately 3,000. It is estimated that by the end of 2015, Russia will have about 25,000 mosques.... In light of these trends... a considerable number of important seats in the Russian parliament will also go into the hands of Muslim leaders. Muslim clerics operate orphanages in Russia as a means of converting children to Islam. If Russia becomes an Islamic nation, it will join other Islamic nations in the desire to eliminate Israel.[89]

Moreover, Russia is presently in a great many alliances with the other nations predicted in Ezekiel's end-time coalition. The Russians have always sided with the Arabs in virtually every skirmish that they have had with the nation of Israel. Showers observes:

During the Cold War, part of Russia's status involved working with Islamic nations to block American influence in the Middle East. For example, it supplied Syria and Egypt with military weapons to use in their wars against America's Middle-East Ally, Israel. One indication that Russia continues that approach in the 21st-century is its supply of weapons to Hezbollah in Lebanon and Hamas in Gaza to use in their wars against Israel. It is common knowledge that those weapons were delivered from Russia via Syria and Iran.[90]

The perpetual siding of the Russians with the Arabs against Israel has been observed by numerous commentators.[91] According to McCall and Levitt, in the 1956, 1967 and 1973 wars, "Russia [was] fully allied with the Arabs"[92] and, "In late October 1973 the American military went on 'Alert' in an announced response to Russian troop movements. It was said that Russia was planning to move combat troops into the theatres of the Yom Kippur War."[93] Rhodes states that "historical records prove ... that during the 1967 Six-Day War, the Russians were poised to attack Israel and had

---

89 Showers, p. 96.
90 Ibid., pp. 94–95.
91 Maughan, pp. 42–45.
92 Thomas S. McCall and Zola Levitt, *The Coming Russian Invasion of Israel* (Chicago: Moody, 1974), p. 38.
93 Ibid., p. 13.

been preparing to do so for a substantial time."[94] In 1982, according to Joel Rosenberg:

> ... then-Israeli prime minister Menachem Begin went public with a story that prior to that time had been known only to the upper echelons of Israeli and U.S. intelligence. The Israeli Defense Forces, he explained, had uncovered a secret but massive cache of Soviet weaponry in deep underground cellars and tunnels in Lebanon that had caught him and his top advisers completely off guard. The weapons appeared to have been pre-positioned by Moscow for the launching of a full-scale invasion of Israel. . . . [95]

Tim LaHaye adds, "One cave near Sidon was literally a Soviet military base with sufficient stores to supply an army of 100,000 soldiers. The Israelis also found maps and documents showing Russian plans to invade Israel on August 4, 1982."[96] He also notes, "Some estimates of eyewitnesses to the network of caverns and tunnels have gone as high as 'military equipment for an army of between 500,000 and a million men,'"[97] and, "In one underground bunker alone, Israeli soldiers captured 70,000 Russian Kalashnikov assault weapons."[98] He adds that all of this "suggests that Israel's assault on Lebanon thwarted a Soviet attack that would have been launched in August—just two months later."[99] In the words of LaHaye, "The question arises, Was Russia planning to use this weaponry for the invasion of Israel prophesied in Ezekiel 38–39?"[100]

For *Rosh* to join with *Persia* in the last days attack that Ezekiel foresaw, an alliance would have to form between *Rosh* and *Persia*, or Russia and Iran. This alliance, in and of itself, is also a very recent development. According to Rosenberg, "Never in the last 2,500 years have Russia and Iran had a

---

94 Rhodes, p. 173.
95 Joel C. Rosenberg, *Epicenter: Why the Current Rumblings in the Middle East Will Change Your Future* (Wheaton, IL: Tyndale, 2006), p. 147.
96 Tim F. LaHaye, *The Coming Peace in the Middle East* (Grand Rapids: Zondervan, 1984), p. 55.
97 Ibid., p. 180.
98 Ibid., p. 181.
99 Ibid., p. 178.
100 Ibid.

military alliance. This caused many a skeptic to think.... There's no way they are going to form an alliance against Israel or anybody else. This just proves the Bible is full of errors."[101] In fact, prior to 1979, Iran was an ally of America, not Russia. Thus, Ezekiel's prophecies seemed inconceivable.

However, everything changed in 1979 with the deposing of the Shah, replacing him with the Ayatollah, and the transition of Iran into a Shiite Muslim country. Today, Iran and Russia find themselves in a cozy relationship with one another exactly as predicted by the sixth-century B.C. prophet. Iran wanted to rebuild its weaponry that it lost during the Iran-Iraq War. Russia, on the other hand, needed money due to the collapse of communism. In other words, oil-rich Iran had money but no weapons. Russia, on the other hand, thanks to its military buildup prior to the Soviet Union's collapse, had weapons but no money. So Russia began selling weapons to Iran in exchange for money. Consequently, it was a match made in heaven, or hell, depending upon your point of view.[102] Thus, as Rhodes notes, "Iran has now become the third-largest recipient of Russian arms with an estimated annual trade of $500 million."[103] Such a scenario could never have never materialized prior to 1979 since the Shah of Iran was an ally of America rather than in a partnership with America's enemy, Russia.

Beyond merely being in a modern alliance with Iran, Russia also finds itself in similar collaboration with other nations mentioned in Ezekiel's end-time coalition. For example, the developing partnership between Russia and Libya (or *Put*) is fascinating to watch. Grant Jeffrey summarizes:

> Russia maintains fourteen major air bases in Libya alone with more than five hundred and fifty Russian combat aircraft.... Russia now has more air force jets in Libya than the total combined air forces of England, West Germany, and France. In addition, Russia has prepositioned a staggering sixteen thousand tanks and armored cars in Libya.[104]

---

101 Rosenberg, p. 104.
102 Ibid., p. 106.
103 Rhodes, p. 45.
104 Grant Jeffrey, *Final Warning: Economic Collapse and the Coming World Government* (Toronto, Ontario: Frontier, 1995), p. 114.

Stories seem to constantly abound in the news explaining the burgeoning relationship between Russia and Libya:

> Russia is prepared to renew military technical cooperation with Libya if the UN Security Council allows it, Russian Deputy Foreign Minister Mikhail Bogdanov said Thursday. Earlier, Libyan authorities expressed hope to continue cooperation with Russia in military training and the purchase of modern weaponry, a 40-year history of collaboration. . . . On April 14, Libyan Prime Minister Abdullah Thinni told Sputnik that Libya plans to ask Russia to help rebuild its military, implementing a number of 2008-era contracts signed between the Gaddafi regime and Russia.[105]

Many other similar alliances could be documented. However, at this point it is sufficient to concur with Ron Rhodes, who well states, "The unique alignment of nations described in Ezekiel 38 and 39 has never occurred in the past, but it *is* occurring now."[106]

Sheba, Dedan and Tarshish?

Our prophetic analysis thus far has only examined the major players in Ezekiel's end-time invasion prophecy. Let us complete our discussion by also observing the role that three minor nations will play in this eschatological drama. Some of the lesser known players in this last-day invasion include Tarshish, Dedan and Sheba. These names are mentioned in Ezekiel 38:13, which states, "Sheba and Dedan and the merchants of Tarshish with all its villages will say to you, 'Have you come to capture spoil? Have you assembled your company to seize plunder, to carry away silver and gold, to take away cattle and goods, to capture great spoil?'"

What are Sheba, Dedan and Tarshish saying here? They are portrayed as merely protesting. They are not depicted as doing anything of real significance to stop the invasion. In other words, they will stage merely a lame protest.

What modern nations are represented by these three ancient names?

105   "Russia Ready to Renew Cooperation with Libya," <http://sputniknews. com/politics/20150416/1020952665.html, April 16, 2015>; Internet; accessed 30 May 2015.
106   Rhodes, p. 90.

The location of Sheba and Dedan are somewhat easy to identify. Consultation with a modern map indicates that the city of Dedan is currently in Saudi Arabia. Sheba could also very well be in Saudi Arabia. Others maintain that Sheba is perhaps a slight distance further north in Yemen.[107] Tarshish, of course, is the place where Jonah fled to in disobedience to God's command to preach to Nineveh (cf. Jon. 1:3). Most believe that Tarshish is modern-day Spain. For example, the *Ryrie Study Bible* indicates that Tarshish "is located in the S of Spain near Gibraltar, 2,500 mi. (4,000 km) W of Palestine [or Israel] and the opposite direction from Nineveh."[108] According to both Brown, Driver and Briggs[109] and Gesenius,[110] Tarshish represents ancient *Tartessus* located in Spain. Interestingly, Ezekiel 38:13 says, "Tarshish with all its villages." Some Bible translations, such as the NKJV, instead render the phrase "Tarshish, and all their young lions." Mark Hitchcock explains why this phrase could actually represent a broader western coalition, including Europe:

> Young lions are often used in the Scripture to refer to energetic rulers. There-fore, the young lions who verbally oppose Gog's invasion are strong military and political leaders who act with Tarshish.... It was in the farthest west regions of the known world, in Spain. As we know, Spain is in modern Europe. Tarshish, or modern Spain, could be used by Ezekiel to represent all of the western nations whom Saudi Arabia in denouncing this invasion.[111]

In sum, Sheba and Dedan most likely represent Saudi Arabia. Tarshish most likely represents Spain as well as a conglomeration of western powers including Europe.

Interestingly, the prophecies regarding Sheba and Dedan, or modern-day Saudi Arabia, now presently fit into the exact prophetic alignment that

---

107 J. Randall Price, "Ezekiel," in *The Popular Bible Prophecy Commentary: Understanding the Meaning of Every Prophetic Passage*, eds. Tim LaHaye and Ed Hindson, Tim Lahaye Prophecy Library (Eugene, OR: Harvest House, 2006), p. 191.

108 Ryrie, p. 1,421.

109 Brown, Driver, and Briggs, eds., pp. 1,076–77.

110 Gesenius, p. 875.

111 Mark Hitchcock, *After the Empire: Bible Prophecy in Light of the Fall of the Soviet Union* (Wheaton, Il: Tyndale, 1994), p. 101.

Ezekiel predicted. Hitchcock explains:

> Does all of this have any relevance to the situation we see in the world today? I think it fits the present world political situation precisely. Who is the one Middle East nation who consistently sides with the West against the radical Islamic elements in that region of the world? The obvious answer is Saudi Arabia — ancient Sheba and Dedan.[112]

More to the point, an interesting headline appeared recently revealing the intention of the Saudi Prince, al-Waleed bin Talal, to "side with Israel" against an invasion of the Jewish homeland instigated by Iran, or *Persia*, and Russia, or *Rosh*. The headline reads, "Saudi prince al-Waleed bin Talal: In case of outbreak of Palestinian uprising I'll side with Israel, Saudi Arabia reached a political maturity to constitute durable alliance with Jewish nation." The article goes on to say:

> According to Kuwaiti Al Qabas daily, the flamboyant Saudi Prince and entrepreneur, al-Waleed bin Talal posited that his country must reconsider its regional commitments and devise a new strategy to combat Iran's increasing influence in Gulf States by forging a Defense pact with Tel Aviv to deter any possible Iranian moves in the light of unfolding developments in the Syria and Moscow's military intervention.... "I will side with the Jewish nation and its democratic aspirations in case of outbreak of a Palestinian Intifada (uprising) and I shall exert all my influence to break any ominous Arab initiatives set to condemn Tel Aviv, because I deem the Arab-Israeli entente and future friendship necessary to impede the Iranian dangerous encroachment," Al Qabas cited the Saudi media tycoon as he is in a regional tour, visiting the other Gulf Arab littoral states.... "... we cannot permit Iran to wreak havoc in our back yard," said the Saudi Prince....[113]

Thus, the right political alignment seems to be in proper position

---

112 Ibid.
113 "Saudi prince al-Waleed bin Talal: In Case of Outbreak of Palestinian Uprising I'll side with Israel, Saudi Arabia Reached a Political maturity to Constitute Durable Alliance with Jewish Nation," <http://www.awdnews.com/top-news/ saudi-prince-al-waleed-bin-talal-in-case-of-outbreak-of-palestinian-uprising-i- ll-side-with-israel,-saudi-arabia-has-reached-a-political-maturity-to-constitute-a- durable-alliance-with-the-jewish-nation-to-lay-the-ground-for-a-peaceful-and- prosperous-middl, October 27, 2015>; Internet; accessed 18 January 2016.

for the fulfillment of the lame protest as a reaction to the Iranian and Russian-led invasion by Saudi Arabia as is predicted in Ezekiel 38:13.

Moreover, if the prior identification of "Tarshish, and all their young lions" with Spain and Europe is accurate, then there are good reasons as to why Europe would protest the prophesied invasion that Ezekiel 38 and 39 predicts. Hitchcock explains:

> The Bible clearly reveals that the great western power in the end times will be centered in the reunited Roman Empire. It is highly probable that Ezekiel used the far western colony of Tarshish to represent the end-times empire of the Antichrist. This is consistent with.... Daniel 9:27 and Revelation 6:2–4. The Antichrist and his Saudi Arabian allies will protest this invasion because the Antichrist will be joined to Israel by the seven-year covenant when Gog moves into Israel like a storm. However, Gog and his allies will completely ignore the protests of other nations and relentlessly storm into the land of Israel. All human efforts to change his mind will be futile because there are unseen powers behind the scenes drawing Gog into the land of Israel.[114]

In sum, Ezekiel's sixth-century predictions concerning the protests by Saudi Arabia and Europe found in Ezekiel 38:13 make perfect sense in light of modern political alignments as well as what the rest of Scripture reveals concerning the end-times scenario.

America?

What about America? What role will she play in this end-time invasion? America would certainly rush to Israel's rescue, would she not? After all, has not America been a long-standing ally of the nation of Israel? Was it not Golda Meir who called Richard Nixon in the middle of the night, in 1973, to ask for help? Dora Von Lehe recounts the story:

> As a young boy growing up, Richard Nixon's Christian (and a Quaker) mother told him that one day he would be in a powerful position,

---

114 Hitchcock, *After the Empire: Bible Prophecy in Light of the Fall of the Soviet Union*, pp. 101–2.

and a situation would arise where Israel and the Jews needed his help. When it did, he was to help them. It is reported that Nixon said he heard the voice of his mother saying these words to him when he responded to the call and plea for help from Golda Meir at 3 a.m. in October of 1973 during what is called the Yom Kippur War. . . . Then came the attacks on October 6, 1973-a coordinated surprise attack on Yom Kippur, the holiest of days in the Jewish calendar and a time when the entire nation comes to a virtual standstill. Even non-observant Jews honor this holyday by fasting, staying home or going to synagogue, and refraining from the use of fire, electricity, and communications systems. Israel could not have been more vulnerable. There had been concern about possible attacks, but until just shortly before the attacks began, "Israeli intelligence was not able to determine conclusively that an attack was imminent." To demonstrate how much Israel was up against: 180 Israeli tanks faced over 1400 Syrian tanks; closer to the Suez Canal, a mere 436 Israeli infantry were poised to fight over 80,000 Egyptian soldiers. The attacks by Egypt and Syria were backed by nine Arab states, as well as the Soviet Union. By the second day, the slaughtering of Israeli troops and destruction of their equipment had been such a blow, Moshe Dayan the minister of Defense, who had been a hero in the Six Day War, started talk about pulling back and even possible surrender. Golda Meir, Prime Minister of Israel, resisted this, but she did have an aid secure lethal pills from her doctor; just in case her Arab enemies prevailed, Meir would take her own life. . . . U.S. Secretary of State Henry Kissinger and Meir's relationship was to say the least a bit rocky. When assistance was requested from him, Kissinger's reported response was to let Israel 'bleed a little.' So, at 3 a.m. Golda Meir picked up the phone and called President Richard M. Nixon and asked for help. It is reported that Nixon heard the prophetic word and the voice of his mother as he listened to Meir. By the time she hung up, Golda Meir had the weapons help her country needed that swung the pendulum to Israel's favor and to bring an end to the Yom Kippur War. . . . To this day, Richard Nixon is highly regarded in Israel. Prime Minister Golda Meir and Nixon kept in frequent touch throughout the ordeal. For the rest of Meir's life, she referred to Nixon as "my president," and said, "For generations to come, all will be told of the miracle of the immense planes from the United States bringing in the material that meant life to our people."[115]

---

115 Dora Von Lehe, "God Uses US Presidents For His Purpose: Israel-Golda Meir and Nixon," <https://www.christianblog.com/blog/revgenlink/god-uses-us-presidents-for-his-purpose-israel-golda-meir-and-nixon/, August 22, 2011>; Internet; accessed 30 May 2015.

Sadly, when you look at the current administration and the current trajectory of our government, we have to wonder if our own president would even take this kind of a call. Beginning with George Herbert Walker Bush, America's 41st president, America's relationship with Israel has become progressively strained. It was Bush who cut off American loan guarantees from Israel to retaliate against Israel's settlement practices. It was also Bush's secretary of state, James Baker, who infamously quipped, "[Expletive] the Jews. They don't vote for us anyway."[116] It seems that with almost every president we have had ever since, both Republican and Democrat, America's once healthy relationship with Israel has unraveled even further. Today, American-Israeli relations are at a historic low. American President Barack Hussein Obama was arguably the most anti-Israel president in American history. If you doubt this claim, note Ben Shapiro's complete timeline of Obama's anti-Israel statements, actions and policies.[117]

Israel does not need America as much as America needs Israel on account of the blessings of the Abrahamic Covenant that are attached to blessing Israel. God in His Word clearly declares that He "will bless those who bless" Israel (Gen. 12:3). Given America's current strained relationship with Israel, our national well-being and future do not look bright. With America turning its back on our once-valued ally Israel, this too fits into Ezekiel's prophetic blueprint. The prophet predicts that Israel will be invaded by this hostile coalition of nations with no nation coming to her aid, including the United States. In sum, every nation mentioned by Ezekiel seems to be finding the proper prophetic orbit that the prophet foresaw coming into existence in the last days.

116   Saul Singer, "George Bush, James Baker, and the Jews," <http://www.jewishpress.com/sections/features/feautures-on-jewish-world/george-bush-james-baker-and-the-jews/2014/10/31/, March 12, 2015>; Internet; accessed 30 May 2015.
117   Ben Shapiro, "A Complete Timeline of Obama's Anti-Israel hatred," <http://www.breitbart.com/national-security/2015/03/20/a-complete-timeline-of-obamas-anti-israel-hatred/, March 20, 2011>; Internet; accessed 30 May 2015.

Israel's Miraculous Survival
from an Overwhelming Attack

Finally, we come to a *third* strategic trend that is also in place, thereby setting the stage for Ezekiel's prophesied invasion. This third trend is that the right scenario must be in place whereby an overwhelming coalition of nations will attack Israel and yet Israel will win against all odds and miraculously survive. In fact, this scenario is already in place with attacks already having happened on many occasions in modern times. Israel has miraculously survived an overwhelming attack against all odds from a coalition of nations during her War of Independence in 1948. This same scenario repeated itself in 1967 during Israel's Six-Day War. The pattern recurred in 1973 during the Yom Kippur War. Nobody bet on the Jews' survival during any of these wars. This similar pattern also seemed to be in place in 1990 during the Gulf War. It is almost as if God is saying, "Get ready! You have seen the dress rehearsal. The main act is now ready to take place."

In other words, the scenario spoken of by Ezekiel is no longer far-fetched but familiar and credible. We are living in the general time period when history has finally caught up with Ezekiel's vision received along the *Chebar* River 2,600 years ago. Every time I review and brush up on the general material in this book it is always out of date. It is not out of date in the sense that these things are becoming unclear, but rather it is out of date in the sense that Ezekiel's scenario is getting clearer and clearer. This said, we have answered the "How?" question by analyzing how the world is currently being set up for the fulfillment of Ezekiel's prophecy through our examination of three strategic trends. Now that we have solved the *Who?*, *When?*, *Why?*, *What?*, and *How?* questions, we will conclude with seven points of application.

7

Seven Points of Application

Application deals with the "So what?" question. Why should we care about all these things? How does a knowledge of these truths impact our daily lives as Christians? Note these *seven* points of application.

Prophecy is Proof of Biblical Inspiration

First, prophecy is proof of Biblical inspiration. Prophecy is history pre-written. Only the Bible declares history in advance because only the Bible was given to us by an all-knowing God. In fact, in Isaiah 48:3–5, God challenges the idols of Isaiah's day and He asks, "Which of them can predict the future?" These verses state:

> I declared the former things long ago
> And they went forth from My mouth, and I proclaimed them.
> Suddenly I acted, and they came to pass.

Because I know that you are obstinate,
And your neck is an iron sinew
And your forehead bronze,
Therefore I declared *them* to you long ago,
Before they took place I proclaimed *them* to you,
So that you would not say, "My idol has done them,
And my graven image and my molten image have commanded them."

We easily could weave this concept of prophetic truth into our evangelism. Prophetic truth, of course, is not the gospel. The ultimate goal of evangelism is to point people to the gospel. However, the concept of prophecy as proof of Divine inspiration is something that can be a conversation starter. I have discovered that the world will give you a millimeter of hearing when you start talking in prophetic terms. Bible readers and believers are the only people with any kind of real answer or explanation as to where things are moving in the world and the Middle East. Thus, we should use this Divinely-given tool to advance the cause of the proclamation of the gospel.

Prophecy Has a Calming Effect on the Believer

Second, prophecy has a calming effect on the believer. It is tempting to look at the *Middle East Meltdown* and lapse into fear. However, when we see things moving in the exact direction Ezekiel predicted, this reminds us that God is in control of a world that seems to be spinning wildly out of control. Rather than seeing things as falling apart, they are actually falling into place. God is sovereign. When we are reminded of this great truth of Divinely determined history, prophecy provides the added benefit of calming us down.

No Need to Fear Rising Islam

Third, we need not fear the rise of Islam. As we watch one moderate government after another toppled and then replaced by another far more radical regime, it is tempting to become fearful and anxiety-ridden.

We see mosques going up constantly. We see that Muslims are repopulating at disproportionately high birth rates. It is tempting to become worried about this. Yet, God is not worried. God is going to bring down Islam just as fast (or faster) as it came upon us in the West. As revealed in Ezekiel 38 and 39, a whole Divine blueprint is in play whereby God will ultimately destroy Islam.

Prophecy Reminds us of God's Faithfulness

Fourth, prophecy is a reminder of God's faithfulness. God has been faithful to a rebellious nation, the nation of Israel, for thousands of years merely on account of His promises to them. Studying God's end-time program for Israel reminds us of His faithfulness to His Word. If God were not faithful to His promises, then Israel should have been eradicated a long time ago. If God is going to be faithful to His wayward nation, then He is certainly going to be faithful to you and to me!

People often debate eternal security. However, one of the greatest arguments that God preserves us and keeps us regardless of our spiritual fruit or lack thereof is by observing His pattern with wayward Israel. Israel has no corner on God. God does "not change" (Mal. 3:6). Hebrews 13:8 indicates that "Jesus Christ *is* the same yesterday and today and forever." Second Timothy 2:13 says, "If we are faithless, He remains faithful, for He cannot deny Himself." If God will be faithful to His apostate nation, then He will be faithful to us as well—in spite of our glaring imperfections. When we study God's faithfulness over these many centuries to the harlotrous nation of Israel (Ezek. 16; 23), eternal security becomes easier to accept.

Keep Your Eye on Israel

Fifth, keep your eye on Israel. Ezekiel 38:12 speaks of the Jews living in the land of Israel as those "who live at the center of the world." Ezekiel 5:5 furnishes the same explanation when it says, "Thus says the

Lord GOD, 'This is Jerusalem; I have set her at the center of the nations, with lands around her.'"

In the mind of God, Israel—the covenanted nation—is the very center of the earth. The Hebrew word translated "center" is literally the navel or belly button, which refers to the center of the body.[118] To the world, Israel is just an insignificant nation standing in the way of modern globalism and progress. However, God does not view Israel in this way. Rather, He views Israel as the centerpiece of the Divine drama as well as the stage of end-time history. Consequently, if we are thinking biblically, we should also be focused upon Israel.

Notice this quote from W.E. Blackstone, who wrote a famous book in 1908 about Christ's return, entitled *Jesus is Coming*. Here, Blackstone observed, "Israel is God's sun dial. If anyone desires to know our place in God's chronology, our position in the great march of events, look at Israel."[119] Consequently, our focus from the Divine viewpoint should be upon the nation of Israel in order to ascertain the times and the seasons in which we are living.

Support Israel

Sixth, we should support Israel. If God's goal is to preserve Israel and Satan's goal is to destroy Israel, we must decide on which side of the spiritual conflict we want to be. I believe that those that move into replacement theology and chop Israel off, saying that she has no future, are taking a side in this conflict. We should speak up on behalf of Israel. We should adopt a theology which is consistent with God's revelation concerning Israel. We should pray for Israel according to Psalm 122:6, which says to "Pray for the peace of Jerusalem."

It is distressing to watch the number of Christians who will support a candidate for office who has a foreign policy of hostility toward Israel.

118   Ludwig Koehler and Walter Baumgartner, *The Hebrew and Aramaic Lexicon of the Old Testament*, trans., M. E. J. Richardson, rev. ed., 2 vols. (Leiden: Brill, 2001), 1:367.

119   William E. Blackstone, *Jesus Is Coming: God's Hope for a Restless World* (New York: F.H. Revell, 1908; reprint, Grand Rapids: Kregel, 1989), p. 238.

The Bible informs us regarding how we should vote and who we should support for higher office. The Bible comments on every issue related to life. It comments on things happening in our culture as well as in the realms of domestic and foreign policy. We should allow its insights to guide us regarding how we vote and how we should engage in practical acts to bless the persecuted Jewish people.

Remember That We Are Living on Borrowed Time

Seventh, we must remember that we are living on borrowed time. Christmas lights, Christmas trees and Christmas songs are all signs that Christmas is approaching. However, they are also signs that Thanksgiving is coming since Thanksgiving takes place earlier on the calendar than Christmas. So the signs of Christmas indicate the even-more-rapidly-approaching celebration of Thanksgiving. More importantly, the signs of the looming Gog and Magog war are perpetual reminders that the rapture, which precedes all of these events, is coming even faster.

Living with this reality should motivate our evangelism. There are people that we all know that need to be reached with the gospel or they will be "left behind" to face the events of Ezekiel 38 and 39 and the rest of the tribulation. Knowledge of these prophetic events and how our world is being prepared to experience them should create a sense of urgency within each of us. Therefore, let us allow these prophetic truths to stimulate us to greater personal holiness (1 John 3:2–3) and evangelistic zeal.

SEVEN POINTS OF APPLICATION

FIRST — Prophecy is proof of Biblical inspiration.

SECOND — Prophecy has a calming effect on the believer.

THIRD — We need not fear the rise of Islam.

FOURTH — Prophecy is a reminder of God's faithfulness.

FIFTH — Keep your eye on Israel.

SIXTH — We should support Israel.

SEVENTH — We must remember that we are living on borrowed time.

One Final Thought

In conclusion, we have thoroughly studied all of the details surrounding the events of Ezekiel 38 and 39, not only by examining and answering *five* standard journalistic questions, but also by learning that knowledge of these events should have a dramatic impact upon our lives.

If you are unclear regarding where you would spend eternity, that issue can be resolved right now by simply believing, or placing your personal trust or reliance, in Christ and His promises and power alone for the safekeeping of your soul and for your eternal destiny.

Jesus paid the full penalty for our sins through His death on the cross. Then He rose bodily from the grave, thereby vindicating His claim to full deity and, consequently, His ability to keep all of His promises. Thus, He has done all the work. By trusting in what He has done for us, rather than what we do for ourselves, we can be assured of the present promise and future promise of eternal life.

In John 5:24, Christ explained: "Truly, truly, I say to you, he who hears My word, and believes Him who sent Me, has eternal life, and does not come into judgment, but has passed out of death into life."

Select Bibliography

Blackstone, William E. *Jesus Is Coming: God's Hope for a Restless World.* New York: F.H. Revell, 1908. Reprint, Grand Rapids: Kregel, 1989.

Brown, Francis, S. R. Driver, and Charles A. Briggs, eds. *A Hebrew and English Lexicon of the Old Testament: With an Appendix Containing the Biblical Aramaic.* Oxford: Clarendon Press, 1907.

DeMar, Gary. *Last Days Madness.* 4th rev. ed. Powder Springs, GA: American Vision, 1999.

_____. *End Times Fiction: A Biblical Consideration of the Left Behind Theology.* Nashville, TN: Nelson, 2001.

Dyer, Charles H. "Ezekiel." In *The Bible Knowledge Commentary: An Exposition of the Scriptures by Dallas Seminary Faculty*, edited by John F. Walvoord and Roy B. Zuck. Colorado Springs, CO: Victor, 1985.

Feinberg, Charles L. *The Prophecy of Ezekiel: The Glory of the Lord.* Paperback ed. Chicago: Moody, 1969. Reprint, Chicago: Moody, 1984.

Fruchtenbaum, Arnold G. *Footsteps of the Messiah: A Study of the Sequence of Prophetic Events.* rev. ed. Tustin, CA: Ariel, 2003.

Gaffney, Frank. *War Footing.* Annapolis: Naval Institute Press, 2006.

Gesenius, Wilhelm. *Gesenius' Hebrew and Chaldee Lexicon.* Samuel Bagster and Sons, 1847. Reprint, Grand Rapids: Baker, 1987.

Hanegraaff, Hank. *The Apocalypse Code.* Nashville, TN: Nelson, 2007.

Hitchcock, Mark. *After the Empire: Bible Prophecy in Light of the Fall of the Soviet Union.* Wheaton, IL: Tyndale, 1994.

_____. *Middle East Burning: Is the Spreading Unrest a Sign of the Times?* Eugene, OR: Harvest House, 2012.

Hitchcock, Mark, and Thomas Ice. *The Truth Behind Left Behind.* Sisters: OR: Multnomah, 2004.

Hoehner, Harold W. "The Progression of Events in Ezekiel 38–39." In *Integrity of Heart, Skillfulness of Hands: Biblical and Leadership Studies in Honor of Donald K. Campbell*, edited by Charles H. Dyer and Roy B. Zuck, pp. 82–92. Grand Rapids: Baker, 1994.

Ikin, Jon. "Downgrading for Armageddon: Does the Bible Suggest a Weapons Downgrade in the Last Days?" *Prophetic Witness*. March 2014, pp. 4–5.

Jeffrey, Grant. *Final Warning: Economic Collapse and the Coming World Government*. Toronto, Ontario: Frontier, 1995.

Jeremiah, David. *What in the World Is Going On? 10 Prophetic Clues You Cannot Afford to Ignore*. Nashville: Nelson, 2008.

Johnson, Philip C. "Cush." In *Wycliffe Bible Encyclopedia*, edited by Howard F. Vos, Charles F. Pfeiffer and John Rea. Chicago: Moody, 1975.

Koehler, Ludwig, and Walter Baumgartner. *The Hebrew and Aramaic Lexicon of the Old Testament*. Translated by M. E. J. Richardson. 2 vols. rev. ed. Leiden: Brill, 2001.

LaHaye, Tim F. *The Coming Peace in the Middle East*. Grand Rapids: Zondervan, 1984.

MacLeod, David J. "The Fifth 'Last Thing': The Release of Satan and Man's Final Rebellion (Rev. 20:7–10)." *Bibliotheca Sacra* 157, no. 626 (April 2000): 201–14.

Maughan, Stanley A. "Selected Expert Perspectives on Ezekiel 38–39 Related to Current World Events with Resulting Influence on Ministry Practices." D.Min. diss., Dallas Theological Seminary, 2012.

McCall, Thomas S., and Zola Levitt. *The Coming Russian Invasion of Israel*. Chicago: Moody, 1974.

McDowell, Josh, and Don Stewart. *Answers to Tough Questions Skeptics Ask About the Christian Faith*. San Bernardino: Here's Life, 1980.

Pentecost, J. Dwight. *Things to Come: A Study in Biblical Eschatology*. Findlay, OH: Dunham, 1958. Reprint, Grand Rapids, Zondervan, 1964.

Piper, John. "Land Divine?: We Should Treat the Israeli-Palestinian Dispute as We Would Any Other." *World*, May 11 2002.

Price, J. Randall. *Jerusalem in Bible Prophecy: God's Stage for the Final Drama*. Eugene, OR: Harves Houset, 1998.

_____. "Ezekiel." In *The Popular Bible Prophecy Commentary: Understanding the Meaning of Every Prophetic Passage*, edited by Tim LaHaye and Ed Hindson, pp. 170-218. Eugene, OR: Harvest House, 2006.

Rhodes, Ron. *Northern Storm Rising: Russia, Iran, and the Emerging End-Times Military Coalition against Israel*. Eugene, OR: Harvest House, 2008.

Rosenberg, Joel C. *Epicenter: Why the Current Rumblings in the Middle East Will Change Your Future.* Wheaton, IL: Tyndale, 2006.

Ryrie, Charles C. *Ryrie Study Bible: New American Standard Bible.* Chicago: Moody, 1995.

Salus, Bill. *Isralestine: The Ancient Blueprints of the Future Middle East Policy.* Crane, MO: Anomalos, 2008.

_____. *Psalm 83, the Missing Prophecy Revealed: How Israel Becomes the Next Mideast Superpower.* La Quinta, CA: Prophecy Depot, 2013.

Scofield, C. I., ed. *The New Scofield Reference Bible.* New York: Oxford University, 1909. Reprint, 1996.

Showers, Renald. *The Coming Apocalypse: A Study of Replacement Theology Vs. God's Faithfulness in the End Times.* Bellmawr, NJ: Friends of Israel, 2009.

Sproul, R. C. *The Last Days According to Jesus.* Grand Rapids: Baker, 1998.

Tan, Paul Lee. *The Interpretation of Prophecy.* Winona Lake, IN: BMH, 1974.

Twain, Mark. *The Innocents Abroad, Complete.* 1st ed.: A Public Domain Book, 1869.

Walvoord, John F. *Israel in Prophecy.* Grand Rapids: Zondervan, 1962.

_____. *The Nations in Prophecy.* Grand Rapids: Zondervan, 1967.

White, Chris. *False Christ: Will the Antichrist Claim to Be the Jewish Messiah?* Ducktown, TN: CWM, 2014.

Yamauchi, Edwin. *Foes from the Northern Frontier.* Grand Rapids: Baker, 1982.

Dispensational Publishing House is striving to become the go-to source for Bible-based materials from the dispensational perspective.

Our goal is to provide high-quality doctrinal and worldview resources that make dispensational theology accessible to people at all levels of understanding.

Visit our blog regularly to read informative articles from both known and new writers.

And please let us know how we can better serve you.

Dispensational Publishing House, Inc.
Taos, NM 87571

DispensationalPublishing.com

CPSIA information can be obtained
at www.ICGtesting.com
Printed in the USA
FSOW02n0019301216
29019FS

9 781945 774003